LOSS AND CHANGE

One of England's most imaginative social scientists, Peter Marris was educated at Bryanston School and Cambridge University, England, where he studied philosophy and psychology. After serving in the colonial administration in Kenya (1953–55), he joined the Institute of Community Studies, London, where for the next seventeen years he undertook research in Britain, America, and East and West Africa, on topics ranging from women's adjustment to widowhood and students' experience of university education to community action in the United States, the social consequences of slum clearance in Nigeria and America, and the development of African businesses. He is currently at the Centre for Environmental Studies, London, and has been a visiting lecturer in urban studies and social planning both at the University of California, Berkeley, M.I.T., and the University of Massachusetts. He is the author of *Widows and Their Families, Family and Social Change in an African City, The Experience of Higher Education, Dilemmas of Social Reform* (with Martin Rein), and *African Businessmen* (with Anthony Somerset).

LOSS AND CHANGE

Peter Marris

ANCHOR BOOKS
ANCHOR PRESS/DOUBLEDAY
GARDEN CITY, N.Y.
1975

Anchor Books edition: 1975
Published originally in hardcover in the United States by
Pantheon Books, and in Great Britain by Routledge and
Kegan Paul Ltd.

ISBN: 0-385-11029-4

CONTENTS

ACKNOWLEDGMENTS

A grant from the Ford Foundation enabled me to take time to write this book. So many friends and colleagues have helped me with their criticisms of drafts of this essay, I will not attempt to name them all here. But I would like to thank Michael Young and Peter Wilmott not only for their help with this book, but for their support, advice and friendship over all the years I was doing the research from which it stems.

INTRODUCTION

Since the argument of this essay began as a reflection on research in which I have been engaged, I can best introduce it by way of the various studies which helped to compose it. These studies had not been designed to develop any consistent theme. The topics ramified over the years—the effects of bereavement amongst widows in the East End of London, slum clearance in Nigeria and America, students' experience of university education, American experiments in social reform, African businessmen. But despite their variety—perhaps even because of it—I began to notice how similar themes had caught my attention in them all. Each was concerned with a crucial transition: bereavement; rehousing, where the new house also implied a new way of life; graduation into an educated élite; transformation of social services to meet the needs of the poor; the pioneering of new business ventures. In each, as I saw it, the anxieties of change centred upon the struggle to defend or recover a meaningful pattern of relationships. A characteristic ambivalence, which I had first noticed in the reactions of the bereaved, seemed always to inhibit any straightforward adjustment. I had evidently been looking at these situations from the same point of view, imposing on them a similar bias of interpretation, and I began to wonder whether this pattern of thought could be articulated explicitly as an analytic framework.

Was there a common thread relating the defensive conser-

vatism of threatened communities or institutions to the distress
of bereavement and the dilemmas of innovators, beyond the
accidental association of ideas that any research career would
generate? It seemed to me that the concept of grieving could be
applied to many situations of change which we would not ordi-
narily think of as bereavement; that whenever people suffered
loss—even though they might also desire change—their reactions expressed an internal conflict, whose nature was fundamentally similar to the working out of grief. Once the anxieties of loss were understood, both the tenacity of conservatism
and the ambivalence of transitional institutions became
clearer.

But this emphasis on loss and grief made spontaneous innovation harder to explain, since innovators often seem to accept the disruption of familiar relationships, for the sake of the
changes they wish to make. Why should people willingly seek
situations which, if my argument was right, must involve them
in the anxieties of loss? To account for this, I have tried to extend the concept of bereavement beyond obvious experiences
of loss to any situation which arouses the same underlying anxieties: the innovator, that is, accepts the strain of change to escape from a more fundamental threat of loss. Thus though the
connection between grief and change was evident in some
cases, it had to be traced also where it is much harder to define,
if the implications of the argument were to be followed out. I
believe it can be traced in ways which are not merely idiosyncratic.

Though the central question arose out of a haphazard
sequence of studies, it reflects a continual issue of sociological
explanation. How can we account for the stability of social institutions in ways which do not seem to deny the likelihood of
change; or explain change without discounting the resilience
of patterns? The idea of bereavement is, I believe, a crucial
link—and a very important link to understand, because it
brings to light aspects of change which we tend to ignore, and
so do much harm to ourselves and others. In this book, therefore, I have tried to develop an argument about the relationship between conservatism, bereavement and innovation
which I hope has some practical as well as theoretical relevance. If it is right, it should influence the way we manage

social changes—both in initiating and responding to them—as some of the examples which follow suggest. But it is not a theory of social change; it applies only to some situations of change, and tries to understand only one aspect of them—the response to loss.

The book begins with a discussion of conservatism, because the argument as a whole depends on the assumption that the impulse to defend the predictability of life is a fundamental and universal principle of human psychology. Conservatism, in this sense, is an aspect of our ability to survive in any situation: for without continuity we cannot interpret what events mean to us, nor explore new kinds of experience with confidence. This first chapter attempts to trace the implications of this deep-rooted and insistent need for continuity. What happens, then, when despite all our endeavours the familiar pattern of life has been irretrievably broken? The rest of the book sets out to explore the implications of bereavement in these terms, starting from the reactions of young widows to their husbands' deaths. This analysis of the way grief works itself out is the key to all that follows; the understanding I have tried to develop should apply not only to such bereavement, but to any situation where the pattern of life has been radically disrupted. There, too, we should find counterparts to grief and mourning—a similar struggle to repair the essential thread of continuity, whose resolution follows a profoundly ambivalent course. The next three chapters illustrate this theme, extending the analogy more and more broadly, from slum clearance— which is not hard to see as a bereavement—to the experience of colonisation and its aftermath, where I believe it can still be traced.

There are kinds of change, as the next chapter discusses, which do not threaten this basic need for continuity of understanding. But if the conservative impulse is so universal, and the disintegration of the familiar pattern of life so traumatic, why should anyone willingly seek changes which do? In the third part of this essay, I have tried to account for innovation in terms consistent with the premises of the whole argument. I believe that we can trace, in the genesis of innovation and its essential purpose, the working out of a social and psychological reorganisation fundamentally similar to bereavement and mourning. Here, too, I have presented the argument mostly through illustrative examples; and since this is the manner of the essay, it needs some justification.

Evidence selected to illustrate an argument cannot of course confirm it, especially when the argument began as an interpretation of that evidence. It would have been an impossible task to review all the vast range of research relevant to the argument I present here. By the diversity of examples, and by seeking out some which seemed at first sight most difficult to reconcile with my framework of interpretation, I have tried to see whether it leads to obvious anomalies of understanding. But the examples are not meant to test the argument systematically, only to bring it to life and show how I have derived it, and how it might be applied. Its usefulness depends on the coherence of the connections I have tried to draw, and whether they enable us to understand better and see more. Since, too, I have used the examples to illustrate the way we respond to loss, I have largely ignored the political and economic causes of loss. I do not mean by this to underrate the influence of power relationships. But the two concerns are complementary rather than contradictory. In the final chapter, particularly, I have suggested some of the political implications I would draw from my argument.

I have tried to use everyday language in an everyday sense. But it may help to explain at the outset how I have used three crucial concepts which are central to the argument—'the conservative impulse', 'structures of meaning' and 'grieving'. Each is intended to refer to a basic aspect of human psychology. By the conservative impulse I do not mean political conservatism, but the tendency of adaptive beings to assimilate reality to their existing structure, and so to avoid or reorganise parts of the environment which cannot be assimilated. Changes in structure seem only to be possible gradually, within the limits of what can be assimilated. I am concerned in this book with the organised structures of understanding and emotional attachments, by which grown people interpret and assimilate their environment. I have called these 'structures of meaning', because in everyday language 'meaning' can include a sense of attachment as well as understanding, as when we say that something 'means a great deal' to someone. It seemed the best

phrase I could find as a shorthand for the complex mental organisation which makes everyone a consistently adaptive being
in the range of environments he or she can tolerate. I hope I
have avoided philosophical problems of the meaning of meaning. Lastly, I have used 'grieving' to refer to the psychological
process of adjustment to loss. As I shall try to show, grieving
reactions are evoked when adaptive abilities are threatened. In
this sense grieving is a more inclusive concept than the obvious, extreme emotional distress which the bereaved may
express. The more or less conventional, institutionalised
expressions of grief I have called 'mourning'.

I hope it will not seem pretentious or egocentric to derive a
synthesis of ideas from my own experience of research. It
seems to me worth asking not only how different observers see
the same topic, but how the same observer sees different topics.
Whatever is consistent in the style of interpretation from study
to study is likely to represent the underlying and most intimate
pattern of thought. If this pattern can be articulated and communicated, it becomes open to critical examination, outgrow-
ing its autobiographical setting.

I
THE CONSERVATIVE IMPULSE

A woman loses her husband; a household is evicted by a slum clearance scheme; the son of a peasant farmer launches a modern wholesale business in his village; a new plan of action sets out to challenge the jurisdiction of established bureaucracies. In each of these situations, a familiar pattern of relationships has been disrupted; and in each of them the disruption seems to provoke a fundamentally comparable reaction. Whether the change is sought or resisted, and happens by chance or design; whether we look at it from the standpoint of reformers or those they manipulate, of individuals or institutions, the response is characteristically ambivalent. The will to adapt to change has to overcome an impulse to restore the past which is equally universal. What becomes of a widow, a displaced family, a new organisation or a new way of business depends on how these conflicting impulses work themselves out, within each person and the relationships of which he is part.

We accept resistance to change as a fact of life. We expect civil servants to be defensive when challenged by innovators, or peasant farmers to react with suspicion to new techniques. We know that children are easily upset by disturbances in the routine of life, and take it for granted that to lose someone you love is deeply distressing. But why? Humans are also the most adaptable of all living creatures—they survive in an extreme variety of social and physical environments, they go through great changes in the course of the most commonplace careers, we scarcely ever live two days exactly alike. In the face of drastic disruption—wars, earthquake, enslavement—the survivors somehow pull themselves together and go on. Why then should we think conservatism natural, and what is its nature?

When we argue about the need for social change, we tend to explain conservatism away as ignorance, a failure of nerve, the obstinate protection of untenable privileges—as if the resistance could be broken by exposing its irrationality. But when we turn from general questions of policy to the experience of people in society as they struggle to maintain their hold on life, the conservative impulse appears more pervasive and profound than simple prejudice or class interest. It is as necessary for survival as adaptability: and indeed adaptability itself depends upon it. For the ability to learn from experience relies on the stability of the interpretations by which we predict the pattern of events. We assimilate new experiences by placing them in the context of a familiar, reliable construction of reality. This structure in turn rests not only on the regularity of events themselves, but on the continuity of their meaning.

This theme underlies everything which follows in this book, since it has, I believe, far-reaching implications for the management of change. But the theme itself can be set out in a few pages. It is evident in the common experience of life, and—once you turn your mind to it—obvious enough. We could not survive even for a day if our physical environment were not predictable. In a television show, for instance, a man repeatedly tries to open a door: each time something different happens. It opens one way or another, it falls on him, it won't open at all, the walls collapse. Like most jokes, the sequence releases an underlying anxiety by parodying it. If things really behaved so capriciously we would be helpless. Hence we insistently impose regularity on events which are never exactly alike nor self-evidently regular. (Even the sunrise, for instance, is not an obviously regular event. It occurs at different times according to the season; in some places it may not rise or set at all for months on end; and it is liable to eclipse.) Confidence in the predictability of our surroundings rests not only on the accident of living—except in dreams—in a consistent world, but on our ability to abstract from particular events the underlying laws which govern them, in ways which are relevant to our human purposes. These physical laws are manmade: they are very different now from what they were a hundred or even fifty years ago; they are different in African tribal societies compared to our own. We can impose widely various interpretations on the physical universe, seeing different meanings in it, and still live well enough. What we cannot do is survive without a system of some kind for predicting the course of events. It does not matter that the system may be false on another system's terms, so long as it identifies experiences in a way which enables people to attach meaning to them and respond.

So the social order evolves from the physical order, as we perceive it. But the principles which determine the predictability of the social environment are even more obviously of our own making than the sense we impose on the natural world. Each of us, to manage our relationships with others, needs to understand their behaviour, so that we know how to respond in our own interest: and we depend on our behaviour provoking in turn more or less the reaction we expected. For instance, a sociologist has described some experiments in which he persuaded his students to flout these expectations in their everyday behaviour ('Studies of the routine grounds of everyday activities', in Garfinkel, 1967). Instead of accepting conventional remarks as usual, the students questioned them, professed not to understand, demanded additional evidence. This improbable behaviour provoked bewildered anger. Dangerously, some of the students played this trick on their own husbands and wives; and it sometimes upset the relationship so much that, even after the experiment had been explained, a tinge of uneasiness and guilt lingered on. The predictability of behaviour is profoundly important, and it depends not only on some shared sense of the meaning of relationships but on conventions of expressing this meaning, which must be insisted on all the more anxiously because they are arbitrary. Children learn this from their parents and apply it obsessively to their own games, handing on from generation to generation forms of verbal play whose wording scarcely changes in a hundred years. (See Opie, 1959.) Throughout childhood, courtship, working life, we elaborate speech, dress, etiquette into subtle, expressive systems of signs whose value depends upon conformity. Each symbolic grammar is a language to express the meaning of relationships—their purposes, expected patterns of interaction, the framework of assumptions about the world into which they fit. Any challenge to convention is likely at first to provoke bewildered resentment. Middle-aged Americans from the Mid-west are outraged by the long hair they see on men students at Berkeley: they cannot interpret this symbolic gesture except as a kind of obscenity thrown in their faces. But in time the styles of dissent too become codified and understandable.

In a political sense, conservatism is an attempt to consolidate established norms of behaviour and the principles which justify them. But in a more fundamental sense, it is a condition of survival in any situation, even for the most radical innovator. We cannot act without some interpretation of what is going on about us, and to interpret it we must first match it with an experience which is familiar. This is an opposite process from the impulse of political conservatism. It is not concerned with regulating relationships to assure their compatibility with traditional principles, but with discovering the principles which reveal their regularity. In daily life, the regularity of social events does not characteristically appear as the expression of a set of rules, but—like the physical world—as an enormous variety of experience in which we learn to find consistent patterns of meaning. Each discovery is the basis for the next, in a series of interpretations which gradually consolidate, with more or less assurance and consistency, into an understanding of life. Hence there is a deep-seated impulse in all of us to defend the validity of what we have learned, for without it we would be helpless.

From earliest childhood, we learn to attach meaning to the things and people about us. We transfer experience from one situation to another, perceived to be essentially alike; and so the circumstances of life become increasingly manageable, as more and more of them can be put into familiar categories. The process begins very early, before a child has any language or power of thought: it begins to smile or cry at circumstances which it recognises as benign or frightening. Since learning builds on what has gone before, the foundation of our sense of the meaning of life is laid in the earliest years, which we cannot recall and therefore cannot re-examine. These are commonplace observations of child psychology; and though schools of psychological theory would disagree about how to explain them, all would agree on the observable nature of this learning process.

I have tried to present the argument in a form which leaves

open most of the controversial problems of the psychology of learning. It does not matter here whether, for instance, motives are conceived as drives which become directed or as patterns of behaviour which become imprinted with relationships to specific objects. Either way, the attachment of feeling and purpose follows a cumulative process of learning, however we interpret its stages.

I think it would be premature to attempt any precise definition of 'the conservative impulse' or 'structures of meaning' in terms of psychological theory, until these theories of human learning are more highly developed. But these ideas can readily be related, for instance, to the developmental psychology of Jean Piaget. He conceives intellectual development as a special case of general principles of biological adaptation, which evolves by the interplay of assimilation and accommodation. Assimilation depends upon the pre-existence of organising structure sufficiently developed to incorporate the experience. The process of assimilation may lead to modifications of structure (accommodation), but only within limits of continuity. As John H. Flavell says (1963, p. 50):

> Assimilation is by its very nature conservative, in the sense that its primary function is to make the unfamiliar familiar, to reduce the new to the old. A new assimilatory structure must always be some variant of the last one acquired and it is this which insures both the gradualness and continuity of intellectual development.

Piaget's research is largely concerned with explaining the development of these cognitive structures throughout childhood, while this essay is concerned with the consequences for mature adults of experiences which they cannot readily assimilate to the structures of interpretation they have developed. The principles are, I think, similar; though I have placed more emphasis on the part emotional attachment plays in the consolidation of these structures, and the parallel development of social structures to protect them.

We grow up as adaptable beings, able to handle a wide variety of circumstances, only because our sense of the meaning of life becomes more certainly consolidated. And it seems that we

survive partly because we impose one meaning with great determination, if need be contradicting facts which to others
seem obvious, and ignoring what is incompatible with our
scheme of things. It does not always work, and it does not
work for anyone all the time. But the experience of psycho-
analytic treatment suggests that it is slow, painful and difficult
for an adult to reconstruct a radically different way of seeing
life, however needlessly miserable his preconceptions make
him. In this sense we are all profoundly conservative, and feel
immediately threatened if our basic assumptions and emotional attachments are challenged. The threat is real, for these
attachments are the principles of regularity on which our ability to predict our own behaviour and the behaviour of others
depends.

The conservative impulse implies, then, an intolerance of
unintelligible events. For if we were to encounter frequently
events on which we could not impose an interpretation, our
behaviour would become alarmingly disoriented. But nothing
becomes meaningful until it can be placed in a context of
habits of feeling, principles of conduct, attachments, purposes,
conceptions of how people behave: and the attachments which
make life meaningful are characteristically specific. They cannot readily be transferred. Purposes which might be satisfied in
many ways become associated with a particular relationship or
setting, and cannot thereafter be detached from it without anxiety.

It seems to me evident why this should be so, from the nature of social leaning. The meaning of events lies in their
consequences for us—good, bad or indifferent. To make sense
of them, therefore, we must be able to discriminate what is
likely to happen in terms of the response we should make. This
presupposes a set of categories, to which to assign events according to their expected outcomes, and a set of purposes, by
which to interpret an appropriate response. Each new event
elaborates and modifies these frames of reference: experience
influences purpose, purposes influence the relevance of experience, both become integrated in more or less comprehensive
structures, where specific expectations and desires are sub-
sumed under general principles of action. But as we grow up,
the structures become more and more difficult to revise, by vir-

tue of their very success. Since new experiences can only be interpreted in terms of what we already know, we are bound to assimilate them to our present understanding if we can; and the longer we live, the less likely we are to encounter events which cannot somehow be incorporated within it, since the experience of a lifetime has refined and elaborated our perceptions into a subtle, wide-ranging and casuistical capacity for assimilating most of what happens to us, and ignoring the rest. A parallel consolidation takes place in the arrangement of our lives, as its meaning becomes elaborated in the particular setting to which it refers, and whose purposes it expresses. Since our ability to cope with life depends on making sense of what happens to us, anything which threatens to invalidate our conceptual structures of interpretation is profoundly disruptive.

The argument as a whole rests on three propositions. Firstly, the construction of meaningful perceptions is cumulative, so that the more fundamental the revisions which have to be made, the more of the structure must be dismantled, and the more disruptive revision becomes. Secondly, the purposive context of meaning seems less open to revision than the ordering of events according to the regularities of experience—we cannot command our feelings, nor reverse the experiences through which our emotional needs have acquired a habit of attachment. Thirdly, meanings are learned in the context of specific relationships and circumstances, and we may not readily see how to translate them to an apparently different context. Nor is the way we have learned to interpret one kind of situation necessarily compatible with the principles by which we interpret another, or even with the way the same relationship is conducted from situation to situation. So long as such situations belong to different parts of our social environment, their incompatibility is not unbearably intrusive. But because of this, our sense of life is bound up in the experience of particular kinds of relationship, and we cannot readily extrapolate from them. As soon as we try, we become perplexed by the mutual inconsistency of our principles, and the poverty of their predictive power apart from the circumstances where we are used to apply them. Faced with the difficulty of detaching our purposes and understanding from the specific situ-

ations where they make sense, we are led to protect the
particular forms with which we are familiar.

Thus the impulses of conservatism—to ignore or avoid
events which do not match our understanding, to control
deviation from expected behaviour, to isolate innovation and
sustain the segregation of different aspects of life—are all
means to defend our ability to make sense of life. Even if we
are wise enough to give up these defences when they become
untenable, we still depend on the continuity of conceptions and
purposes whose stability as organising structures bring novelty
within the grasp of our understanding. Given that this context
of meaning is founded at the beginning of life, and develops
from the first through relationships with adults whose own experience is formed by the society in which they grew up, the
meanings we discover must be, in part, those that our parents
discovered before us. The continuity of this context represents
for an individual his identity; for a society its cultures; and for
mankind, perhaps, the half-hidden outline of a universal philosophy. It is necessarily conservative in the sense that it can
only change by reformulation. Whatever happens, the continuity of past and present must be preserved; and to revise the
principles by which we have interpreted the past is a far more
arduous and impenetrable task than to make what happens
now conform to them.

THE LIMITS OF CONSERVATIVE ADAPTATION

All this I hope is evident. But what it implies for situations of
social change may seem less obvious. In the first place, conservatism and adaptability must be interdependent. For the
readiness to react to new kinds of experience depends on the
ability to assimilate them to familiar principles. Just as, in
the prediction of physical events, mastery of the environment
rests on abstracting regularities from unique events, so social
survival rests on holding to laws of human behaviour which a
man or woman may apply wherever they find themselves.
These are moral laws as much as laws of social science, since
above all we need to understand situations in terms of what is
right and proper to do. And they are, within limits, arbitrary,
since the workable principles of human conduct are widely

variable. The ability to comprehend social situations depends on the stability of these laws, for unless our sense of the meaning of behaviour remains the same from time to time and place to place, we have no basis on which to act. But if we cannot formulate this meaning independently of particular relationships, the range of circumstances we can handle is very limited. Hence those who hold their principles of life to be absolute, universal and unchallengeable may survive in situations of extreme uncertainty, where the more open-minded are destroyed by their inability to derive any intelligible regularity from events around them.

In an account of his experiences in a Nazi concentration camp, for instance, Bruno Bettelheim (1961) describes how the prisoners reacted to circumstances which were made deliberately unpredictable. With cruel psychological insight, the camp guards frustrated any reliable accommodation to the prison régime by the capriciousness of their behaviour: a man might be punished if he did what he was told as well as if he did not. Eventually, to Bettelheim's observation, any personality was bound to disintegrate under such treatment, falling into an apathy which extinguished life. But those who survived best seemed to be the two most ideologically dogmatic groups in the camp—the Communists and the Jehovah's Witnesses.

The same principle underlay recruitment to the British Colonial Service, from its establishment early in this century until the Second World War. (See Heussler, 1963.) District officers were typically posted to country stations where there might be no other European. They collected taxes, administered justice, and undertook simple economic reforms amongst a people whose traditions, language and conventions of behaviour were altogether alien. But the Colonial Service did not train anthropologists, nor teach its administrators native languages. Nor did it seek out sensitive and imaginative men who would readily understand their subjects. On the contrary, it consistently recruited the most conventional, middle class, stolid Englishmen it could find, and sent them out without any training at all. These sons of clergymen and army officers, from minor public schools, did very well in practice, within the limits of the task they were set. They were incorruptible, sure of themselves, and confident of their purposes. They imposed

their own conception of life without self-doubt, and so were
seldom at a loss: they expected their subjects to behave like
children—unreliable but responsive to just control. On the
whole, the people they governed found such predictable
masters easy to deal with.

Most impressive of all, perhaps, were the Victorian mis-
sionaries who worked, like the Hinderers, in African kingdoms
many years before the establishment of British rule. They had
no companions of their own country, their lives were insecure,
they were surrounded by customs of human sacrifice and in-
fanticide which revolted them. Many died after a few years
from disease. Yet their journals are remarkably serene. They
seem always to have been sure what they were doing, however
great the day to day disappointments.

This sense of the power of survival of intransigent identities
pervades the comedy of Charles Dickens, whose novels—
perhaps more than any others in the English language—
express a brooding awareness of profound social changes. 'It is
a world of change,' exclaims the absurd Mrs Chick in *Dombey
and Son*. 'Anyone would surprise me very much . . . and
would greatly alter my opinion of their understanding, if they
attempted to contradict or evade what is so perfectly evident.
Change! . . . Why, my gracious me, what is there that does
not change! Even the silkworm, who I am sure might be sup-
posed not to trouble itself about such subjects, changes into all
sorts of unexpected things continually.' But, characteristically,
the lady herself does not change. Like all Dickens's comic
figures, she remains indestructibly herself. So with the retired
Major, for ever calling his own name in evidence of his
unchangeable nature; and the sea captain stranded ashore,
navigating the city of London like a full-rigged ship; and the
ancient Regency belle. Each is given an identity, exactly
defined by turn of phrase, manner of dress, a stance before the
world which never varies. They are absurd, because they impose themselves with such insolence on the events around
them, blandly oblivious of everything which does not suit their
purpose. But they are also reassuring: for those in the novel
with whom we are invited to identify are by contrast lost—
orphans who cannot find themselves until they have recovered
their true parents. The structure of *Dombey and Son* repre-

sents an allegory of social change where, against the background of a London whose familiar landmarks are being torn apart in confusion and squalor, only those who cling intransigently to their prejudices can survive. They are absurdly inept: but those who see this absurdity are condemned to a tormented search for the meaning of their own lives.

These instances are extreme, and emphasise to the point of parody only one aspect of adaptability. The counterpoint to certainty of purpose is certainty of knowledge. In the concentration camp, Bettelheim also survived, and he was not a religious or political fanatic. He describes himself rather as unsure of his beliefs—a sceptical Freudian psychologist to whom political radicalism had sometimes seemed a more fundamentally important means of change. But he was a sensitive observer. He describes how he was once in need of treatment for an infected hand. The prisoners reported for treatment to a guard, who dismissed or accepted their complaints at whim, without much regard for their needs. Most prisoners tried to win the guard's sympathy, pleading their illness. Bettelheim foresaw that this behaviour was exactly what a young Nazi would despise as weak and self-pitying. Instead, he presented his need in the most matter-of-fact way: the infection was preventing him from working efficiently, the guard could decide what action was called for. This was much closer to the guard's own stereotype of manly, disciplined behaviour, and he passed Bettelheim to the hospital for treatment. By extending his psychological insight, Bettelheim succeeded in regulating his relationship with the guard, and made it predictable.

If, then, consistency of purpose is one means of mastering events, the power of empathy is another: if you understand enough about other people, you can foresee how they will respond, and so govern their relationship with you in their terms as well as your own. The traditions of the Colonial Service were inadequate to meet the problems of rapid economic and political development after the war, because they had refused to cultivate this understanding. In Kenya, for instance, the administration never really grasped the nature of African nationalism, but clung obstinately to its preconceptions. In the eyes of district officers, Africans were children, themselves be-

nign teachers, and the 'true' African leaders men who—like
school prefects—accepted this tutelage. When the expectations
derived from this conception were continually disappointed,
the administration only defended it by more far-fetched rationalisations, elaborating a myth of collective psychological
breakdown which led it into a disastrous and irrelevant policy
of brain-washing (see Rosberg and Nottingham, 1966). So
Kenya stumbled with much bitterness, cruelty and mutual misunderstanding towards Independence.

A consistent interpretation of life is not therefore necessarily
adaptive for either people or institutions. It can end in a wilful
insistence on mistaken notions which becomes tragically destructive. Adaptability seems to depend, rather, on the interaction of two contrasting qualities. Without confidence in the
continuity of our purposes and sense of the regularity of social
behaviour, we cannot begin to interpret the meaning of any
event. But unless we are also ready to revise our purposes and
understanding, we may be led to actions which are fatally misconceived. In the everyday interpretation of a social environment, however, the testing of reality is far less clear cut. Our
own purposes and attachments are a crucial part of the meaning of events; we refer everything that happens to them, as the
underlying determiners of relevance. If we once doubt them,
the system threatens to disintegrate. But these purposes and attachments are neither wholly verifiable by experience, nor
wholly independent of it. It makes sense to ask 'do I really
love?' 'do I care or believe?' reviewing the quality of our relationships. But the answer cannot be found by observation
alone. In part we discover what we intend, but in part we can
only assert it: and this element of will, of choice—the arbi-
trariness underlying the meaning of our lives—makes the
verification of our understanding an ambiguous process. At
what point, if any, should we change our assumptions, if our
expectations of life are continually disappointed? Neither martyrs nor pragmatists are evidently right, on any terms but their
own.

Predictability is related to control. We cannot control the
physical world without discovering its laws, but we can control
our social world, more or less, by imposing laws upon it. Eve-

ryone, however oppressed, has some power of social control
—if only a silent refusal to accept the assumptions of others.
Control by authority has to contend with control of information, with the power of irresponsibility to evade arguments
about consequences, with the choice of self-destruction rather
than compliance. Hence we can never be sure when to surrender to the evidence of failure and when to resort more deter-
minedly to whatever means of self-assertion we can command.
We follow an intuitive moral empiricism whose basic impulse
is conservative. It becomes explicit only in those who struggle
to articulate a comprehensive philosophy, and live by it from
day to day: and this implies either an exceptional rigidity of
conduct, or an exceptional ability to abstract universal principles of behaviour—or both.

Resistance to change is, then, as fundamental an aspect of
learning as revision, and adaptability comes as much from our
ability to protect the assumptions of experience, as on our
willingness to reconsider them. The whole argument can be
summarised in these terms:

1 Survival depends on being able to predict events, with
enough reliability to isolate failures of prediction and ultimately explain them. (Playing our chances can be enjoy-
able, of course, but only so long as the risks are calculable
or trivial.)
2 The probable consequences of events are only predictable
if the events can be related to a context of learning which interprets them.
3 Since a social event is a relationship between oneself and
others—a matter of action as much as a matter of fact—it
can only be understood in terms of one's own purposes,
sympathies and antipathies as well as learned experience of
the regularities of human behaviour.
4 The context of meaning evolves from earliest childhood,
and becomes so structured and integrated that it cannot in
time be radically changed without fear of psychological
disintegration.
5 Our ability to handle the changing environment relies,
therefore, upon conserving the fundamental structure of
meaning each of us has grown up to.
6 The continuing viability of this structure of meaning, in
the face of new kinds of experience, depends upon whether

we can formulate its principles in terms abstract enough to apply to any event we encounter; or, alternatively, on whether we can ignore or prevent experiences which could not be comprehended in terms of it (experiences, that is, where our expectations would be repeatedly and bewilderingly unfulfilled). The first is an extension of learning, the second a constriction of experience: both seek to make life continuously intelligible. In times of change, social scientists and fanatics alike come into their own.

The impulse to preserve the thread of continuity is thus a crucial instinct of survival. But its characteristic expression is more anxiously intuitive than conscious or deliberate. We know that our principles of action are shaky: we mistake our purposes, contradict ourselves, fail to communicate, are baffled by the way others respond. We are always trying to learn and reformulate, searching for a more reliable order in a past we have betrayed or a future we have yet to realise. But the search is always directed to consolidating our interpretation of life, and everything contradictory threatens to undermine what has been so patiently built up. We have to retrieve our misconceptions without undermining the basic structure of thought and attachment from which any reinterpretation must rise. We face this predicament whenever change is disruptive: if events contradict crucial assumptions about our world of experience, they threaten to overwhelm the structures of thought on which we depend to assimilate and adapt to life.

The argument applies in part to any form of learning, in the sense that without some continuity we cannot speak of learning at all. But it is the way continuity of social meaning rests on consistency of purpose and attachments, on respect for arbitrary conventions and means of control which reinforce the conservatism inherent in all adaptation. Much learning does not involve this subtle interplay of experience and intention. A boy learns chemistry, for instance, by being taught the first principles, guided through a series of experiments, and having them explained to him. The knowledge is revealed: he does not, at this elementary stage, have to make his personal interpretation of its meaning for him. Similarly, a peasant farmer can be taught an entirely new set of agricultural techniques.

This kind of knowledge can also be radically revised and re-taught, without causing great anxiety except to those who have identified themselves with a particular theory. So long as a system of knowledge can be presented as a self-contained, limited structure of ideas, it can be reviewed with detachment. But social understanding, even when it concerns something trivial —such as conventions of dress—is part of a set of principles which pervade every aspect of life: the more it is thrown in doubt, the more painfully difficult any action becomes. And social understanding can seldom be acquired through revelation—since it involves purposes and attachments embodied in the unique experience of each individual life. Religious claims to revealed truth do not, I believe, contradict this. For the truth revealed in the Bible or the Koran is as hard to interpret, as open to argument, as overlaid by commentary and revision, as any other view of life; and religious fundamentalism is only one extreme form of the conservative impulse. Certainly, many people report experiences akin to revelation—a sense of serenity, wholeness and understanding; but these experiences do not seem to present any ideas that can be used afterwards until they have been assimilated to some familiar structure of thought.[1] The only social understanding which is primarily revealed is, I think, in fiction. Here the author provides the interpretation, invalidating within the pages of the novel the possibility of any event he or she has not created: and its readers can explore safely worlds of experience very different from their own. But once they see the book as a commentary on their world, it loses its privilege to define the meaning of imaginary events on its own terms. Social understanding is therefore by its nature more idiosyncratic, more dependent on the continuity of meaning in the personal experience of life, and so less open to the presentation of received ideas than other kinds of knowledge.

[1] See Abraham Maslow (1968) on 'peak' experiences. I think the same would be true of drug experiences. See, for instance, Timothy Leary (1968), where he shows, explicitly, how people's interpretations of drug experiences depend on their personality and the setting, and, implicitly, how his own interpretation changed over the years.

CHANGE AS LOSS AND GROWTH

Even if the conservative impulse is as pervasive as I have suggested, it does not follow that every reaction to change must be defensive—either warding off a threat to the assumptions of experience, or attempting to restore their essential validity in the face of disruptive evidence. I do not mean to imply that all growth and learning is a succession of forced innovations: that children only grow up because their biological maturation, and the social demands upon them, repeatedly banish them from the familiar world they understand. This would be a perversely negative account of growth—every frog a bereaved tadpole, every butterfly a frustrated caterpillar. For though children regress to earlier patterns of behaviour when they cannot cope, and adolescents are ambivalent in their seach for maturity, they also look forward eagerly, curiously and impatiently to their future, bored with achievements that come too easily. As the years go by, the social demands for further changes may become less pressing, and the energy to explore less; accumulated frustrations wear confidence away. But I do not think the conservative impulse itself is incompatible with growth. It seeks to consolidate skills and attachments, whose secure possession provides the assurance to master something new.

Despite the anxiety of venturing into the unknown, the process by which maturation provokes change is not fundamentally disruptive. The anxiety can be dominated, just because the thread of continuity has not been broken, and can always be given a reassuring tug. So, for instance, a healthy one-year-old child, exploring a strange room, returns from time to time to its mother, exchanges glances with her, enjoying her presence as a secure base from which to set out again on its adventures. As he or she grows up, in John Bowlby's words 'first the child, then the adolescent, and finally the young adult moves out in a series of ever-lengthening excursions. . . . Each step follows the previous one in a series of easy stages. Though home ties may attenuate they are never broken.' (Bowlby, 1970.) Thus the self-confidence of maturity is not a rejection of support but an ability to turn for reassurance when need arises, trusting that it will be met. The confirmation that more primitive wants are securely satisfied renews confidence to confront the uncertainties of growth. Conversely, if these wants have never been fully met, growing up does indeed become a succession of bereavements; the grown person is a banished child with forged papers of maturity.

Conceived in this way, the idea of growth does not contradict the assumption of a conservative impulse. If there is a hierarchy of needs, and the urge to explore new kinds of satisfaction is only released when we feel confident that more basic needs are assured, then spontaneous growth follows from the consolidation of familiar patterns of expectation. The defensive reactions of conservatism are latent, because no threat to the established structure of meaning provokes them. Then a healthy person looks for new ways to use energy—deepening understanding, extending skills, discovering more abilities. The process is evidently constrained by physical maturation: an athlete, a mathematician, a lyric poet reach and pass the peak of these achievements long before their lives are over. But it is at least plausible to suggest that the quality of understanding— the wisdom of feeling and experience—will continue to grow in those whom the defeats of life have not driven at last into a defensive habit. The same seems to be true of collective endeavours: a science or technology, an artistic or intellectual tradition evolves from generation to generation, bored with its secure achievements, until the possibilities of growth in that direction are exhausted. Here, however, the distinction between growth and bereavement is less easily drawn, because one person's adventure is another's loss. The engineer who extends the power and range of his machines may unwittingly destroy the livelihood of a community, as the explorer destroys the way of life of the people he discovers for his nation.

Different kinds of change can be discriminated in terms of this balance between continuity, growth and loss. First, many changes are incremental or substitutional: the purposes they seek to satisfy and the pattern of expectations remain essentially the same. To buy a new car, wear a new fashion, move house or take a new job may represent simply alternative means of meeting familiar needs, or something better but like.

The continuity of life is unbroken. In practice, these incremental changes can turn out to be more disruptive and disturbing than foreseen: moving house or job involves losses for which, after all, no substitute is immediately identifiable. But the change is routine, in the sense that the reorganisation seems compatible with the established meaning of life, and adds nothing much to it. Second, there are changes which represent growth. Here, too, familiar purposes and expectations are not disrupted, but incorporated within a broader understanding or range of interests. The changes may mean a great deal to whoever initiates them, but they do not threaten the integrity of what has already been learned. A growing person is confident enough to explore new experiences just because the basis of understanding seems secure. Looking back, he or she may acknowledge the immaturity of former purposes, the naivety of expectations: but what has been learned since subsumes them. The sense of continuity is still unbroken. Third, change may represent loss, either actual or prospective, from death or from the discrediting of familiar assumptions—a crisis of discontinuity. And from this arises both innovation and despair.

When a pattern of relationships is disrupted in any way for which we are not fully prepared, the thread of continuity in the interpretation of life becomes attenuated or altogether lost. The loss may fundamentally threaten the integrity of the structure of meanings on which this continuity rests, and cannot be acknowledged without distress. But if life is to go on, the continuity must somehow be restored. When the loss is irretrievable, there must be a reinterpretation of what we have learned about our purposes and attachments—and the principles which underlie the regularity of experience—radical enough to trace out the thread again. To do this, the loss must first be accepted as something we have to understand—not just as an event that has happened, but as a series of events that we must now expect to happen, and a retrospect of earlier events whose familiar meaning has now been shadowed by our changed circumstances. The conservative impulse will make us seek to deny the loss. But when this fails, it will also lead us to repair the thread, tying past, present and future together again with rewoven strands of meaning.

Thus the nature of any change turns on the relationship between continuity of purpose, and continuity of meaningful circumstances. When novelty is consistent with our purposes and the way we are used to interpret life, the change is merely substitution or improvement. Change as growth comes from imposing new purposes on circumstances whose meaning has not been disrupted. Bereavement follows from the disintegration of a meaningful environment without any change of purpose—though out of bereavement a new sense of purpose may emerge in time. In reality, we are likely to perceive the changes we encounter as all these at once—part substitution, part growth, part loss—in varying degrees: and the collective experience of change is even harder to discriminate in these terms, as it bears on people so differently. But though the distinctions are abstract, I think they help to clarify the relationship between bereavement and change, and to place it amongst other aspects of the processes of change.

If we can discriminate the element of bereavement, then much that otherwise seems irrational and frustrating in the response to change will become clearer. This is the theme of my enquiry. The chapters which follow set out to show how an understanding of bereavement can help to explain a crucial aspect of many processes of change, which are experienced as a threat to the adaptive resilience of our interpretive structures. Some of the examples are concerned with individual adjustment, some with groups, some with society at large. I believe the conflicts inherent in these processes, and the way they play themselves out, can be seen as variations of the same fundamental effort to reconstruct a viable sense of meaning. Its most extreme and obvious expression is grief for the death of an intimate companion. The next chapter, therefore, begins by analysing the grieving of widowhood, as the clearest model of an internal struggle which appears again and again, in transmuted form, in response to many kinds of loss.

II
BEREAVEMENT

Of all the changes which beset a lifetime, bereavement is characteristically the change we are least prepared for, and the hardest to accept. Collectively, society is used to death, and has at least some laws, conventions, beliefs for dealing with it. But individually, death—or the onset of a fatal illness—is seldom predictable, and when it comes, those whose lives were intimately involved with the dead are faced by a radical disruption in the pattern of their relationships. When someone dies the bottom seems to fall out of the lives of their most intimate companions. The person on whom so many purposes turned, to whom so many pleasures, conflicts, anxieties related, is suddenly gone. Bereavement presents unambiguously one aspect of social changes—the irretrievable loss of the familiar. And since it is a common experience in every society, the reaction to bereavement is perhaps the most general and best described of all examples of how we assimilate disruptive change. If we can understand grief and mourning, we may be able to see more clearly the process of adjustment in other situations of change, where the discontinuity is less clear-cut.

A mother of two young children, whom I interviewed in the course of a study of widows in London, gave this account of her husband's death, and her reactions to it, twenty months afterwards:

'He was making a little noise is his throat. He turned round on his back and lifted his hands, and folded his arms across his chest. He didn't speak or say a word. He was so cold. I got out of bed and slipped a coat and cardigan on, and went to the door. The milkman was there, and he said "Are you all right missus?" I asked him to come in and look at my husband, so he jumped over the wall, and knocked next door. I don't remember much after that. . . . The ambulance came, and on the post mortem it says he died on the way to hospital, but I feel sure he died in bed beside me.

'I did not see the doctor again until the Wednesday after. I believe he felt guilty. I was walking up and down, and he said, "Mrs. Stewart, Mrs. Stewart, please stand still," and put his hand on my arm. I said, "Don't touch me." He said he couldn't have done anything for him, but I said "You could have done something"—I had to tell him that—"I believe you're afraid of me." He said, "Mrs. Stewart, believe me I sympathise with you greatly." I said, "I don't want your sympathy." My mother was there and she says I acted like a madwoman.

'The minister from the church used to come every day while his body lay there. He used to talk to me—well, you have to think about it. He was so kind, I felt different when he was here. You could talk to him more than anyone else. . . . But you can't help asking "Why did it have to be him?" There are lots of young men about who are horrible to their wives, bad fathers. It's so unfair, it doesn't seem possible. I've got used to it now, but even so it doesn't seem as if you can understand it . . .

'At first I just couldn't understand it. It didn't seem real. It just didn't seem possible, he was such a strong man. I just couldn't cope for a long while, there was nothing to do for it. My sister and the minister told me to pull myself together, but I said "What for?" They said I had to for the children, but I still felt there was nothing to do for it.

'It was a month before we got used to his not coming in. Sheila used to say, "I wish Daddy would hurry up," and I'd say "Oh Sheila! don't say things like that," and then she'd burst into tears when she realised what she had said. When the kettle would be on, and I heard a van draw up outside the house, I've gone to open the door, thinking it must be him. He used often to drive up like that, and call for a cup of tea. He liked his tea in a pint mug, and I've still got it. In the night I've heard him cough—he used to give a little cough, and I'd get up. One night I even called out to him "Tommy, you're coming to bed," because he used to sit there reading. I've often felt him here. I don't know if I'm fumbling in describing him to you, but I think for him. I think, he'd like that or, what would he say to this . . .

'I've only just sort of—I still feel dreadful. My Mum says

I'm different entirely, and the children say "You don't laugh
like you used to." I'm beginning to pull round a bit now, but
it took over a year. Even when we went on holiday, I wasn't
there.' (Marris, 1958, pp. 11–12.)

GRIEF

These reactions are typical of severe, normal grief, as it has
been systematically observed in Britain and America. At first
the bereaved are restless, and cannot sleep; they feel
exhausted, have no appetite, and may suffer symptoms of chest
and digestive illness, headaches, rashes or rheumatism. The
shock of bereavement may numb them for a while. It takes
time to realise the fact of death, and the bereaved find themselves acting as if the dead person were still alive—making his
tea, waiting for him to come home from work, thinking of
news to tell him. They may still hear, or less commonly see,
the dead, and these illusions can be frightening, making them
fear for their sanity. Geoffrey Gorer quotes the experience of
a widower (1965, p. 58):

'I was upstairs after the wife died and I was watching television for the first time after she died; and all of a sudden I
could see my wife as plain as anything, sitting in one of
these chairs. I flew downstairs and never went into that
room again.'

These senses of the dead person's continuing presence, the
dwelling on memories, dreams, illusions, talking with them in
imagination, alternate with sharply painful reminders of loss.
The prevailing mood is apathetic—a feeling of the aimless futility of life, which sometimes leads to thoughts of suicide. The
bereaved tend to withdraw from all relationships. At the same
time, they are troubled by guilt and hostility. They may blame
the doctor, the hospital or themselves for the death, or the
dead for deserting them, and rage against the world for the
injustice of their bereavement. They anxiously look back over
their relationship with the dead, trying to reassure themselves
that they did everything they could to make him or her happy,
or struggling wtih remorse for remembered neglect or un-

kindness. They may become irritable, or overwhelmed with hostility towards everyone who is not suffering as they are. Sometimes this bitterness leads them to repudiate their religion, as a promise of the goodness of life which has been betrayed.

The typical signs of grief can be summarised, then, as physical distress and worse health; an inability to surrender the past —expressed, for instance, by brooding over memories, sensing the presence of the dead, clinging to possessions, being unable to comprehend the loss, feelings of unreality; withdrawal into apathy; and hostility against others, against fate, or turned in upon oneself. The intensity and frequency of these reactions naturally vary with the relationship to the dead, with circumstances and personality, but the general pattern seems remarkably consistent, at least in recent British and American observations. Erich Lindemann (1944) concluded from an American study of 101 bereaved, some of whom had lost a relative in a fire disaster, that the characteristic signs of grief amongst them were somatic distress, preoccupation with the image of the dead, guilt, hostile reactions and loss of patterns of conduct. In my own study of 72 London widows, who ranged in age from twenty-five to fifty-six, 31 said their health had deteriorated, 57 had found it hard to sleep, and 47 said they had experienced a loss of contact with reality—through inability to realise their loss (17), obsessive memories (5), a sense of their dead husband's presence (36), or by behaving as if he were still alive (15). Forty-four had withdrawn into apathy, 27 said they had withdrawn from people, and 13 that they had tried to escape from all reminders of their loss. Eleven spoke of a need to blame, 13 of resentment and 8 of guilt. Murray Parkes (1965) has compared these figures with the grief reactions of fourteen women of similar age, who were undergoing psychiatric care for symptoms of mental illness following on a recent bereavement. The pattern of their grief was very similar: most signs—apathy, insomnia, loss of contact with reality—appeared with the same frequency. But they found it more difficult to accept their loss, blamed themselves much more often, and others somewhat more. Geoffrey Gorer (1965), from his interviews with 80 men and women who had recently lost a relative, describes similar reactions, except for guilt and blame—which he suggests may be because his respondents were mostly mourning 'natural deaths in the fullness of time', while in my own and several other studies, the deaths were premature and unexpected.

Thus, though there are few systematic studies of grief, their findings confirm that grief is a sickness with a consistent pattern. Murray Parkes comments (op. cit., p. 1):

> Of all the functional mental disorders almost the only one whose cause is known, whose symptomatology is stereotyped and whose outcome is usually predictable is grief. That grief is a mental disorder there can be no doubt, since it is associated with all the discomfort and loss of function which characterises such disorders.

It is a mental wound, which heals slowly and leaves scars. Once the numbness of shock has worn off, the pain is at first acute; gradually the attacks of sharp distress become less frequent, the despair duller, until at last grief is recalled only on rare occasions. Normally, the acute phase of grief seems to last for several weeks if the loss is severe, only slowly and intermittently abating for as much as a year or more. The widows I interviewed seemed to take about two years to recover from their grief—and some said, 'You never get over it,' in the sense that the experience had permanently changed them. The death of a husband under fifty is perhaps the hardest bereavement to accept in British society—such deaths are usually unexpected, and the relationship the most important in a woman's life. Grief does not always last so long. But it seems, from all the studies, that it is a process which must be worked out, from shock through acute distress to reintegration. If the bereaved cannot work through this process of grieving, they may suffer lasting emotional damage.

From clinical observation, the three commonest patterns of reaction, where the process seems abortive, are delayed, inhibited and chronic grief. In the first, the bereaved express little sorrow. They set about reorganising their lives with practical busy-ness, and accept their loss calmly. Sometimes the morbid nature of this busy activity betrays itself by haste and poor judgement, or is even perversely self-destructive. It often seems hollow, as if concern for everything but the superficial day to day management of life had been suppressed. But much later, often in response to a less important or trivial loss—the death of a more distant relative, a pet—the bereaved person is overwhelmed by intense grief. In the second pattern, however, grief is permanently inhibited. It becomes displaced into physical disorders or neurotic conditions not recognised as grief, and never finds full expression: this seems to happen most often to children or old people who have been bereaved. Third, chronic grief is by contrast an indefinite prolonging of the acute phase of yearning and despair. The bereaved settle into a lasting depression—anxious, irritable, apathetic and obsessed by memories. 'Mummification'—as Geoffrey Gorer calls it—is perhaps a milder form of the same reaction: 'The most notorious exemplar of mummification in recent English history is Queen Victoria, who not only preserved every object as Prince Albert had arranged them, but continued the daily ritual of having his clothes laid out and his shaving water brought.' (Gorer, 1965, p. 79.) The dead person's possessions, room, home are treated as a shrine in which that presence is embalmed—life frozen at the moment of loss, as Miss Faversham, the jilted bride in *Great Expectations,* sits forever in her wedding gown at the ruins of her marriage feast.

Each of these patterns of reaction seems to exaggerate some aspects of normal grief—the impulse to escape from everything connected with bereavement, the worsening of physical health, the despair or refusal to surrender the dead. And in each, counter-balancing impulses have been suppressed. The process of normal grief seems to be a working out of conflicting impulses: while in abortive grief patterns, the conflict is never resolved. This conflict is crucial to an understanding of grief and mourning. But it also suggests a model of adjustment which, as I hope to show, can be applied to other situations of change.

The behaviour of the bereaved is characteristically ambivalent: they may be desperately lonely, yet shun company; they may try to escape from reminders of their loss, yet cultivate memories of the dead; they complain if people avoid them, embarrassed how to express their sympathy, yet rebuff that sympathy irritably when it is offered. They may insist that there is no longer anything to live for, while they hurry back to their jobs, take care of their children, move house with practical efficiency. This ambivalence seems to express a complex conflict between the claims of the past and the future, which makes the present almost unbearably painful. The bereaved refuse to surrender the dead, reviving them in imagination—they talk to them, do things they would like, think of all the things they did together, continue familiar routines. But when the illusion falters, they experience afresh the realisation of their loss. At the same time, they try to turn away from everything that will revive their distress—condolences, memories, places associated with the dead. But then, if for a while they can forget their loss, they begin to fear that they have betrayed the relationship. Could it, after all, have been so important, if they do not remain inconsolable? Does the ability to forget, even for a few hours, expose the secret insincerity of their love? 'All the petty irritations, harboured grievances, moods of rejection and disillusion that may have marred their relationship with the dead, present themselves as hostile witnesses to torment the bereaved. Nothing imperfect in the relationship can now be changed or forgiven, and no lingering resentment can be expressed without disloyalty. Hence the bereaved sometimes cling obstinately to their grief and idealise the dead, in expiation of a latent sense of guilt.' (Marris, 1958, p. 27.)

Thus each of the two fundamental impulses of grief—to return to the time before death, and to reach forward to a state of mind where the past is forgotten—is checked by the distress it arouses, forcing the bereaved to face the conflict itself. The struggle to master this conflict for a while drains all their vitality. Some cannot bear to admit the conflict, and some cannot resolve it, but most become reconciled in time.[1]

---

[1] 'So long as the response systems are focused on the lost object there are strenuous and often angry efforts to recover it; and these efforts may continue despite their fruitlessness being painfully evident to others, and sometimes also to the bereaved himself. In this phase are sown, I believe, the seeds of much psychopathology. When the mourning process proceeds healthily, however, the response systems gradually cease to be focused on the lost object and the efforts to recover it cease too. Disorganisation of personality accompanied by pain and despair is the result. This is the second

This process of reconciliation is crucial to the outcome of bereavement, and its phases are institutionalised in the mourning customs of most societies in one form or another.

Traditionally, full mourning in England would begin with the shuttering of the house, and the hanging of black crêpe, while the dead person was laid out in his or her old home. The funeral procession itself was decked with as much pomp as the family could afford, or its sense of good taste suggested. Thereafter, the nearest relatives wore black for several months, and then half mourning for a while, gradually adding quiet colours to their dress. They lived in retirement, avoiding public pleasures or any show of gaiety until their mourning was over. Cheerful events in the family, such as a marriage, were postponed a while: and a widow or widower could not decently consider proposals for remarriage until the mourning had run its term. But the term was limited by convention, and the social pressure which would condemn too hasty a return to normal life also reproved an overprolonged indulgence of grief. At first, the family might visit the grave often, laying fresh flowers there; in time they would go less and less, but a visit on the anniversary of the death might become a perennial ritual of remembrance. Such customs symbolise the stages of grief: at first the household withdraws, shutting out life; then, by the ceremony of the funeral, it emphasises its concern for the dead; then, through the months of mourning, it gradually comes to terms with its loss. And when the period of mourning is over, it can take up the thread of life without guilt, because the customs of society make this its duty. At the same time, the observance of these rituals sustained a relationship with the dead: it was done for their sake, as much as for the world. Conventional Christianity allowed the bereaved to imagine

phase. The third phase completes the work of mourning and leads to a new and different state; during it a reorganisation takes place, partly in connection with the image of the lost object, partly in connection with a new object or objects.' (Bowlby, 1961, pp. 319–20.)

that the dead looked down from Heaven, saw the flowers on the grave, and appreciated them. Thus the relationship was not broken abruptly, but attenuated through all the acts that turned the harshness of death into the gentler sorrow of laying to rest. Yet these acts also acknowledged death—they related to one who had died, not a pretence of a living person.

In most societies, the stages of bereavement are clearly articulated by custom. Grief seems to be a universal human response to loss, and though we cannot be sure that it provokes the same reactions everywhere, irrespective of a society's culture, the mourning rituals described by social anthropologists in widely different societies seem to reflect similar underlying tensions. The bereaved may be expected to show violent distress, and be formally restrained. They may withdraw from social life into a period of seclusion. The dead may be treated for a while as if they were still a living presence: or this presence may be feared—as the widows I interviewed were disturbed by hallucinations of their dead husbands—and prevented by rituals which bar the ghost from harassing the living. Death may be blamed upon some unknown assailant, who must be sought out so that it can be avenged. Whether grief is to be displayed or hidden; whether the funeral ceremonies are austerely sorrowing or enlivened by food and drink; whether the dead are at once laid to rest or expected for a while to return, a shadow at the boundary of the living world, the rites of mourning seem to interpret in their own way the evolution of a conflict. Death must be acknowledged, so that life may continue. The continuity may be expressed through a gradual attenuation of the social identity of the deceased—as, for instance, when the children born to a widow for a year or more after her husband's death are still considered his. Or it may be expressed by a more abrupt retying of the broken threads of relationship. But the conflict must still be worked out: the continuity of life cannot be re-established until the nature of the disruption has first been made clear. The loss must be insisted upon, otherwise the value of the lost relationship may seem disparaged, threatening all such relationships which still survive: but it must also be made good, and the bereaved must be led to re-establish themselves within society. Thus the rites of mourning serve to disentangle the dead from the living, and knit the web of relationship together again.[1] But it must be done with fine discrimination; for while the dead must be dismissed, the values they represented in all their relationships must be preserved.

Grief, then, is the expression of a profound conflict between contradictory impulses—to consolidate all that is still valuable and important in the past, and preserve it from loss; and at the same time, to re-establish a meaningful pattern of relationships, in which the loss is accepted. Each impulse checks the other, reasserting itself by painful stabs of actuality or remorse, and recalling the bereaved to face the conflict itself. Grieving is therefore a process which must work itself out, as the sufferer swings between these claims, testing what comfort they might bring, and continually being tugged back to the task of reconciling them. If the process is aborted, from too hasty a readjustment or too unchecked a clinging to the dead, the bereaved may never recover. The rites of mourning can help to articulate this process, lightening the burden of responsibility on the bereaved themselves.

THE RESOLUTION OF GRIEF

This analysis of grief and mourning still leaves some crucial questions unanswered. How is the conflict resolved? and why should it be so painful? Both the obstinacy of the conflict and the distress it arouses remain puzzling, as Sigmund Freud first

---

[1] Jack Goody (1962, p. 46) summarises the funeral ceremonies of the Lo Dagaa, for instance, as:

B The performance of rites that *aggregate* (1) the deceased to from the living, that is, from the bereaved, from the various groups and quasi groups to which he belonged, from the community, and from his roles, offices, property, and rights over women; and (2) the bereaved from the other members of the community.

A The performance of rites that *separate* (1) the deceased his ancestors and to the Land of the Dead; and (2) the bereaved to the community from which they have been temporarily separated, a process that includes the redistribution of the relatively exclusive rights.

noticed in his essay on 'Mourning and melancholia', (Freud, 1925 edn, vol. IV, p. 154):

> The testing of reality, having shown that the love object no longer exists, requires that all the libido should forthwith be withdrawn from its attachment to this object. Against this a struggle of course arises. It has been universally observed, that a man never willingly abandons a libido position, not even when a substitute is already beckoning to him. . . . Why this process of carrying out the behest of reality bit by bit, which is in the nature of a compromise, should be so extraordinarily painful is not at all easy to explain in terms of mental economics. It is worth noticing that this pain seems natural to us.

Even when the conflict itself is understood, why should it appear so desperate?

Although it seems natural to grieve for the loss of someone or something you love, love does not explain grief. The intensity of grief does not vary with the intensity of love, but is often greater when the feeling for the dead person was mixed. Grown men and women do not usually grieve deeply for the death of their parents, though they may still be very fond of them. We have words for many moods relating to the absence of what we love—sadness, nostalgia, pining—which do not describe grief. The fundamental crisis of bereavement arises, not from the loss of others, but the loss of self.

Certain characteristic phrases recur in the interviews with the widows I met, which seem to express more than simply apathy—'I lost all interest', 'I went dead', 'even when we went on holiday I wasn't there', 'when the bottom has fallen out of your life . . .', 'I had nothing to live for . . .'. These words imply more than the loss of a relationship, however important. Everything has gone—as if bereavement had destroyed them, and they were mourning their own death. When the dead person has been, as it were, the keystone of a life, the whole structure of meaning in that life collapses when the keystone falls. Think of a married woman of about forty: her life is centred on her home, and its pattern is largely determined by her relationship to her husband. Most of her purposes, her important anxieties, resentments, satisfactions, involve that relationship.

The meaning of her life is constructed about it.[1] When a widow says life has no meaning any more, she is expressing a literal truth, for the relationship which principally defined who she was and what she had to do is gone. This is true of an unhappy marriage as well as a happy one, so long as she had not already begun to extricate herself from it. The intensity of grief is related to the intensity of involvement, rather than of love. Children cannot at first provide a continuing sense of purpose, because her relationship to them has always included their father, and cannot keep its familiar pattern without him. The one set of relationships whose meaning is not affected by her loss is her job: and this, I think, is why the widows I interviewed tended to return to work as soon as they could. It was the one place where they could be their old selves again.

To say that life has lost its meaning is not, therefore, just a way of expressing apathy. It describes a situation where someone is bereft of purpose, and so feels helpless. Familiar habits of thought and behaviour no longer make sense. Nor can one escape from this distress by adopting new purposes, since—as I discussed in the first chapter—purposes are learned and consolidated through a lifetime's experience, becoming embodied in the relationships which sustain them. They inform the context of meaning by which life is interpreted, and so new purposes remain meaningless, until they can be referred to those which have gone before. This, I suggest, is why the practical busy-ness of those who do not grieve seems hollow and unsound. They appear to have found new purposes, but these purposes have no roots in their past, and represent a disintegration of identity more lastingly damaging than the painful retrieval of purpose from the wreck of dead hopes.

A sense of continuity can, then, only be restored by detaching the familiar meanings of life from the relationship in which they were embodied, and re-establishing them independently of it. This is what happens in the working through of grief. At first, a widow cannot separate her purposes and un-

---

[1] I am thinking of a marriage where a woman follows the conventional expectation of subordinating her career to her family's needs: and one of the consequences must be to make bereavement more totally disruptive for a widow than a widower.

derstanding from the husband who figured so centrally in them: she has to revive the relationship, to continue it by symbols and make-believe, in order to feel alive. But as time goes by, she begins to reformulate life in terms which assimilate the fact of his death. She makes a gradual transition from talking to him 'as if he were sitting in the chair beside me', to thinking what he would have said and done, and from there to planning her own and her children's future in terms of what he would have wished, until finally the wishes become her own, and she no longer consciously refers them to him. So, too, she recasts her relationship to her children, becoming mother and father to them, incorporating her husband's part in their upbringing as an aspect of herself. In the course of this process she will probably change, in personality, in patterns of behaviour, in what she expects from life. But the change will be gradual enough to sustain a continuity of meaning.

Thus grief is mastered, not by ceasing to care for the dead, but by abstracting what was fundamentally important in the relationship and rehabilitating it. A widow has to give up her husband without giving up all that he meant to her, and this task of extricating the essential meaning of the past and reinterpreting it to fit a very different future, seems to proceed by tentative approximations, momentarily comforting but at first unstable. For a while she may not be able to conceive any meanings in her life except those which are backward-looking and memorial, too tragic to sustain any future. In time, if all goes well, she will begin to formulate a sense of her widowhood which neither rejects nor mummifies the past, but continues the same fundamental purposes. Until then, she will often be overwhelmed by feelings of disintegration.

C. S. Lewis has published a diary of jottings (1961), written while he was grieving for the death of his wife, which show something of how a sophisticated and religious man struggled with this task. At first he is preoccupied with the symptoms of grief. 'No one ever told me that grief is so like fear,' he begins, 'the same fluttering in the stomach, the same restlessness, the yawning. I keep on swallowing.' He feels apathetic: 'Except at my job—where the machine seems to run on much as usual—I loathe the slightest effort. Not only writing but even reading a letter is too much. Even shaving. What does it matter now

whether my cheek is rough or smooth?' He can find no
consolation in religion. 'Meanwhile, where is God? . . . go to
Him when your need is desperate, when all other help is vain,
and what do you find? A door slammed in your face, and a
sound of bolting and double bolting inside. After that, silence.
You may as well turn away. . . .' At the same time, he notices
an impulse to escape from grief. 'There are moments, most
unexpectedly, when something inside me tries to assure me
that I don't really mind so much, after all. Love is not the
whole of a man's life. I was happy before I ever met H. I've
plenty of what are called "resources". People get over these
things. Come, I shan't do so badly. One is ashamed to listen to
this voice but it seems for a little to be making out a good case.
Then comes a sudden jab of red-hot memory and all this
"commonsense" vanishes like an ant in the mouth of a furnace.'

After a while, the mood of the writing changes—more engaged with despair, less detached. The loss has come home to
him. He is obsessed by memories of his wife, but clinging to
them seems to distort them, so that she slips further away, the
more anxiously he tries to recall her. 'Already less than a
month after her death, I can feel the slow, insidious beginnings
of a process that will make the H. I think of a more and more
imaginary woman. . . . Is what I shall still call H. to sink
back horribly into being not much more than one of my old
bachelor pipe-dreams? Oh my dear, my dear, come back for
one moment and drive that miserable phantom away.' And he
exclaims bitterly, 'What pitiable cant to say "She will live forever in my memory". *Live?* That is exactly what she won't do.'
This impulse to hold on to the reality of her being leads him to
ask where she is now, what their relationship meant in the
scheme of life, and so to his idea of God. 'What chokes every
prayer and every hope is the memory of all the prayers H. and
I offered and all the false hopes we had. Not hopes raised
merely by our own wishful thinking; hopes encouraged, even
forced upon us, by false diagnoses, by X-ray photographs, by
strange remissions. . . . Time after time, when He seemed
most gracious He was really preparing the next torture.' He
struggles with a sense of God as cruel and indifferent to human
love, at best unintelligible. 'Finally, if reality at its root is so

meaningless—or putting it the other way round, if we are such total imbeciles—what is the point of trying to think about God or about anything else?' His next note is a self-rebuke. 'Why do I make room in my mind for such filth and nonsense?' But the rage against God recurs, side by side with self-reproof, and a continual worrying at the meaning of his marriage, at the meaning of death. Nothing has yet been resolved: 'And grief still feels like fear. Perhaps, more strictly, like suspense. Or like waiting; just hanging about waiting for something to happen. It gives life a permanently provisional feeling. It doesn't seem worth starting anything. I can't settle down.'

But a few pages later, he notes the first glimpse of returning peace of mind. 'Something quite unexpected has happened. It came this morning early. For various reasons, not in themselves at all mysterious, my heart was lighter than it had been for many weeks. . . . And suddenly at the very moment when, so far, I mourned H. least, I remembered her best. Indeed it was something (almost) better than memory; an instantaneous, unanswerable impression. To say it was like a meeting would be going too far. Yet there was that in it which tempts one to use these words.' This reassurance that the memory of his wife will not fade, become corrupted and sentimentalised—that as he recovers from grief, he will recall the past more clearly, not betray it—quiets his impulse to destroy revengefully the foundations of his religious faith. 'And so, perhaps, with God. I have gradually been coming to feel that the door was no longer shut and bolted. Was it my own frantic need that slammed it in my face?'

Now he begins to realise the nature of bereavement. 'I think I am beginning to understand why grief feels like suspense. It comes from the frustration of so many impulses that had become habitual. Thought after thought, feeling after feeling, action after action, had H. for their object. Now their target is gone.' Later he discovers that even experiences unconnected with his wife have lost their meaning. He revisits some of his bachelor haunts. 'Every horizon, every stile or clump of trees, summoned me into a past kind of happiness, my pre-H. happiness. But the invitation seemed to me horrible . . . for this fate would seem to me the worst of all; to reach a state in which my years of love and marriage would appear in retrospect a charming episode—like a holiday—that had briefly interrupted my interminable life . . . I could almost believe it had happened to someone else. Thus H. would die to me a second time; a worse bereavement than the first. Anything but that. Did you ever know, dear, how much you took away with you when you left? You have stripped me even of my past, even of the things we never shared.'

The diary ends with a reconciliation. He has an experience of his wife's presence which is 'incredibly unemotional', 'just intelligence and attention'—'yet there was an extreme and cheerful intimacy. An intimacy that had not passed through the senses or the emotions at all.' He interprets this as evidence that the dead may survive as 'pure intelligence'—at once their essential selves and an aspect of God—and this helps him to re-establish the continuity of life. He can protect the memory of his marriage from the corruption of sentimentality and secure its importance to him, by merging his relationship to his wife in a more generalised sense of spiritual communion. She is at one with God, and so all the thoughts, feelings and actions once directed to her still have a target in the vision of God. Or so the diary implies—it ends when it has served its therapeutic purpose, but probably before the conflicts of grief had been fully resolved. The religious thought is not spelled out, but it seems to represent a symbolic abstraction and generalisation of all that his wife meant to him as part of an awareness of God.

As a writer on the interpretation of Christian faith, C. S. Lewis involves his religious beliefs more intimately in the working out of grief than most bereaved, since they are a central part of his life. But the diary illustrates the normal process of grief only more explicitly because the self-critical, introspective Protestant tradition within which he writes provides a religious language adapted to the intellectual articulation of profound personal conflict. His grief seems typical, progressing from numbness through despair to attempts at reintegration. He reproaches himself repeatedly with the self-centredness of his thoughts: yet it is, indeed, his own identity which must be retrieved and reconstituted. Again and again, the diary returns to the search for continuity—in the values his marriage embodied, in his faith—and concludes as the past is once again able to inform the present with a valid meaning.

The working out of a severe bereavement represents, as a personal crisis, a general principle of adaptation to change. Life becomes unmanageable, because it has become meaningless. The context of purposes and attachments, to which events are referred for their interpretation, has been so badly disrupted by the loss that it at first seems irreparable. Not that the social environment itself has become unpredictable. The bereaved soon learn to understand the embarrassed overtures of condolences, the awkwardness that stilts old friendships, the changes in their status. There are practical affairs to settle in conventional ways. It is themselves they no longer understand, and hence they cannot foresee how to live to any purpose. They go through the motions of living, but they cannot see why it matters to them any more that they do this or that. And the reasons why it still matters can only be rediscovered in the context of purposes and attachments which death has torn up. There is no other basis of understanding, because no one can substitute another's experience for his own. The consoling formulas urged by friends seem glibly impertinent, even when the bereaved in the end adopt something like them. The meaning of life can only be reformed, piece by piece, from the intimate fragments of personal experience.

The severity of grief depends, then, on the degree of disruption: and it can be at least crudely predicted from the emphasis which a society places upon different relationships. A person learns from his culture where she or he is expected to commit themselves most, and their life will be built around these commitments. So, for instance, in modern industrial societies, the death of husband, wife, child, parent, brother or sister or friend roughly represents a declining order in the severity of bereavement, between childhood and old age.[1] In general,

[1] In both childhood and old age, grief reactions seem to be modified. Bereavement is less of a traumatic disintegration of identity, because in old age the context of life has shrunk, and in childhood it is still so much in the process of development. But the consequences of bereavement may be even more serious for children than adults, since the disappointment is embodied so early in the

women seem more vulnerable than men, because their lives are conventionally more bound up in personal relationships. A man's job is usually an important but separate aspect of his identity, segregated from his family and less dependent on intimate personal ties. These generalisations would, of course, need to be qualified by the circumstances of any individual pattern of attachments. And they would not hold for a different culture. In a society where, for instance, the perpetuation of the patrilineage is the central purpose of life, a father's loss of his son may seem the hardest bereavement of all. Yet the loss of anyone we care about seems to evoke at least a moment of grief—perhaps because it reminds us of the insecurity of all our attachments.

BEREAVEMENT, LOSS AND CHANGE

Bereavement is the most unarguable, and at its most severe, the most ill-prepared of all the adjustments to loss with which we are commonly faced. Even when it is foreshadowed by a fatal illness, most families postpone the work of grief until their fears are confirmed. Even those who have the courage to broach the subject rarely believe that the dying should have to confront their own death (though if it is possible to talk to them about the family's future, involving them in the task of adjustment, the continuity may be greater and bereavement less traumatic). For the most part, coming to terms with the loss begins only after it has happened. The most closely comparable situation is probably the breakdown of a marriage, where husband or wife deserts unexpectedly what, to the other, seemed a secure relationship. Dennis Marsden writes (1969, pp. 116–17):

> The mother's emotional bonds with the father did not snap cleanly with the parting. Almost half the mothers, many of whom had completely lost touch with the father, had a sense of longing for him. . . . It was evident that a

formation of their understanding of life. The grief reactions of old people are discussed in Stern, Williams and Prados (1965). Gorer found the death of a grown child to be as upsetting as loss of a young husband or wife.

sizeable minority of women persisted, in spite of evidence to the contrary and sometimes for many years, in thinking they would somehow be reunited with their children's father. The descriptions of broken marriages and illegitimate births suggest that these were women for whom the final parting had been principally the husband's or father's decision or primarily of his making, one-sided, unexpected, and therefore somehow premature. This group included most of those whose husbands (legal or common-law) had deserted. But also there were women who felt their hand had been forced when they divorced their husbands not for violence but for associations with other women or for persistent non-support. Older unmarried mothers who claimed they had been engaged also suffered lasting disturbances when the relationship ended. Analogies with widowhood, where by contrast there was definitely not the remotest possibility of renewing the relationship with the husband, must not be carried too far. Yet there was a striking similarity shown in the attitudes to death by some widows whose husbands had died suddenly or after long spells away in hospital. . . . As with the broken marriages there was somehow a 'failure to take leave', the ending of a relationship which was for the wife still in full flower. And where the children's father suddenly disappeared or deserted, his spiritual 'death' for the wife left an aftermath strikingly like bereavement.

When the breakdown of the marriage can be foreseen, the adjustment to loss is partly, at least, prospective: the moment of parting may not then initiate a process of mourning, because both husband and wife have already disengaged themselves from the relationship. But if mourning properly refers only to a retrospective adjustment, the essential task of grief must be worked out whenever there is a crucial loss—a prospective equivalent of mourning. The meaning of life must be retrieved and reformulated, so that it can continuously survive the relationship which may no longer contain it. In a breaking marriage, this conflict will work itself out by withdrawal, by one partner trying to impose on the other his or her concept of the meaning of the relationship, by self-blame and abortive mutual reformulations, by accusations and mutually destructive impulses of revenge, by nostalgic returns in search of a lost happiness together. And even after the breakdown, an intimacy may survive it which the couple can never share with anyone else. A part of their identities remains bound up in each other, to be revived whenever they meet. At the same time, in the immediate aftermath of divorce, there may be a sense of liberation from any commitment—a promiscuity or indulgence of superficial interests—which seems to resemble the hollowness of delayed grief. Thus the impulses to preserve the relationship in the face of loss, and to abandon it without a backward glance, work themselves out in divorce as in bereavement, with the same risk that the conflict may never be resolved.

This analysis of grief and mourning has been concerned with situations of loss which we recognise as painful. But by the same argument, a similar process of adjustment should work itself out whenever the familiar pattern of life has been disrupted. For once the predictability of events has been invalidated—whether from collapse of the internal structure of purpose, or of our ability to comprehend the environment—life will be unmanageable until the continuity of meaning can be restored, through a process of abstraction and redefinition. From the example of bereavement, this process seems likely to evolve through the gradual resolution of a conflict between attempts to retain the past, and to escape altogether from its consequences, by which a viable reinterpretation is reached. Even changes which we scarcely think to involve loss may be analysable in similar terms.

Marriage, for instance, is almost as sweeping a change in the pattern of relationships as bereavement, though it is not so final and breaks the continuity less. Courtship can be seen as mourning in reverse—the process runs backwards. It begins from more or less indeterminate desires for emotional security, a home, children, fully adult status. Courtship is the gradual commitment of these purposes to a particular relationship, and it proceeds, like mourning, by reinterpreting them to fit new circumstances. But where, in mourning, purposes and attachments have to be retrieved from a specific context and generalised again, in courtship they are made concrete and embodied. At first it may be only a tentative, noncommittal exploration, with all the charm of a day-dream. But as it grows more serious, it tends to become more conflict-ridden. At times too much of oneself seems to have been abandoned or distorted to

make the relationship possible, and there is an impulse to retreat, to recover the true self whose fancy was free. Yet at the
same time, too much has already been committed to extricate
oneself without distress. At this point in a serious love affair, its
breakdown threatens to arouse intense grief, because the lovers
have already begun to organise their lives about an ideal of
absolute and deep commitment to each other. The fear of betrayal, of a bereavement that can only be more damaging the
more either makes a commitment without reciprocal assur-
ances of loyalty, creates a circular anxiety. But if all goes well,
courtship ends where bereavement begins, in the organisation
of essential purposes and attachments which give meaning to
life around a specific relationship, which absorbs and defines
them.

The fascination of love stories arises, I think, from this
process of self-realisation: they dramatise the search for the
meaning of life at every level from sentimental wish-fulfilment
to the profoundest moral speculation. Social change can be a
love story, too—in the career of a reformer, a revolutionary,
an entrepreneur. But just as the bride's mother may weep at a
wedding, what is a love story for one may mean bereavement
for another. Even the bridegroom, by convention, holds a
wake for his bachelor days on the eve of his marriage. Change
appears as fulfilment or loss to different people, and to the
same person at different times. In either aspect it presents some
common features: the need to re-establish continuity, to work
out an interpretation of oneself and the world which preserves,
despite estrangement, the thread of meaning; the ambivalence
of this task, as it swings between conflicting impulses; the need
to articulate the stages of its resolution; and the risk of lasting
disintegration if the process is not worked out. The outcome
therefore depends upon the ability to face the conflict and find
a way through it: the particular terms in which it is resolved
are accidents of personal history. If this analysis can be applied
more generally to situations of change, where the reactions
may be collective or institutional as well as personal, then the
outcome of social changes, too, may depend at least as much
on the management of this process of transition, as upon the
objectives of reform.

III
SLUM CLEARANCE

In his paper 'Grieving for a lost home', Marc Fried has drawn an explicit comparison between bereavement and a social change—the destruction of a neighbourhood and dispersal of its residents. He studied the reactions of families moved from the West End of Boston under an urban renewal scheme, and concluded (1963, p. 151) that:

> for the majority it seems quite precise to speak of their reactions as expressions of *grief*. These are manifest in the feelings of painful loss, the continued longing, the general depressive tone, frequent symptoms of psychological or social or somatic distress, the active work required in adapting to the altered situation, the sense of helplessness, the occasional expressions of both direct and displaced anger, and the tendencies to idealise the lost place. At their most extreme, these reactions of grief are intense, deeply felt, and, at times, overwhelming.

Altogether, about half the 250 women and 316 men he studied said they had been severely depressed or disturbed for a while, and another quarter had been more mildly upset. A quarter of the women were still very depressed two years after they had moved, while a fifth had taken over six months to recover their spirits. The unhappiest exiles described their loss in similar phrases to the bereaved: 'I felt as though I had lost everything', 'it was like a piece being taken from me', 'something of me went with the West End.'

The rehousing of these predominantly Italian families was more carelessly handled than in later clearance schemes. The Boston Redevelopment Authority at that time took only a casual responsibility, and the residents themselves were so suspicious of all representatives of the society beyond their familiar streets—even those drawn from the West End—they could not organise in defence of their interests. (See Gans, 1962.) They were therefore helpless to prevent or soften an expropriation from which they foresaw no benefit. But a sense of bereavement often accompanies the working out of a slum clearance scheme. Some of the families moved from the East End of London to a suburban estate complained in interviews with Michael Young and Peter Willmott of loneliness and the coldness of their new neighbours: wives would sit at home crying, or wander disconsolately back to their old haunts. (See Young and Willmott, 1957.) Even when they enjoyed the amenity of their new houses, they might still feel ill at ease in a setting which, for all its material advantages, did not yet belong to them. In Lagos, Nigeria, where part of the old city was torn down, residents complained bitterly 'it seems like being taken from happiness to misery', 'I fear it like death', and the evictions provoked riot (see Marris, 1961).

What makes slum clearance a kind of bereavement? Even in the West End of Boston, some families were glad of the opportunity to move. Once the sickness for the old home has worn off, people may become equally attached to their new surroundings.[1] The reactions to clearance run all the way from eagerness to escape, through transient nostalgia to lasting grief. If we can understand a change of home, like bereavement, as a potential disruption of the meaning of life, we may be able to see more clearly who will suffer grief, and what might help them to retrieve a sense of purpose. For some, rehousing will represent the realisation of a social status and way of life with which they already identify. For others, it will be, once the strangeness has worn off, a recreation of what they valued in their former neighbourhood. But for some, it may be a profound disturbance from which they never recover. And

[1] Long-standing residents of the Dagenham Estate, in the London suburbs, recalled their dismay when they were first moved from more central districts 35 years before: 'It was terrible for the first two years away from Mum. I longed to be back in Hoxton.' But they were now very well settled on the estate, which had established a strong sense of a comfortable working-class community. See Willmott (1963).

such tragedies are, I believe, more likely, the more slum clearance is used as an instrument of social change, not merely physical development; and the more it is directed against groups in society, whose non-conformity with the ruling values seems to stand in the way of progress.

From this point of view, the slum clearance scheme I studied in Lagos was an object lesson in the inevitable frustration and cruelty of exploiting housing as a means to more fundamental reforms. Not that the redevelopment authority was unconcerned with the social implications of its plan. It had to answer repeated protests against the hardships it caused—by breaking up family groups, isolating old people, bankrupting businesses disrupted by relocation—and tried to relieve them. Nor were the residents it dispossessed unresponsive to the need to adapt and change their city. They had long acquired the city dweller's skill in improvising their own use of buildings designed for another purpose. Both residents and planners were struggling to resolve the tensions inherent in Nigerian society, while maintaining the continuity and coherence of their sense of life. But because these issues had become identified with the fate of buildings, all their complexity was reduced to a single, dramatic act of destruction. If we trace how traditional relationships had evolved in modern Nigerian society, it becomes clear how sensitively the old parts of the city incorporated this adaptation and contained its ambiguities; and how discordant was the design of the rehousing estate. In particular, the redevelopment scheme implied a radical reinterpretation of the meaning of marriage. By setting out its consequences for this relationship alone, the futility of manipulating change by the logic of physical design becomes apparent.

MARRIAGE AND THE STREETS OF LAGOS

Central Lagos expressed, in the use of its spaces, a distinctively Nigerian response to the opportunities and risks of life in a commercial capital, which had been evolving over a century. The way people understood the obligations of marriage, their corresponding emphasis on wider bonds of kinship, and the importance of a wife's earnings to the viability of this pattern of relationships represented together an adaptation of pre-

colonial society. As marriage lost the protection of some traditional sanctions, women sought other guarantees against aban-
donment and hardship, which only gradually and largely
unconsciously changed its meaning. The slum clearance
scheme disrupted this subtle evolution, exposing its latent tensions. To show how the conflict over slum clearance reflected
incompatible conceptions of life, each embodied in a physical
setting, we need to look back to the traditions of marriage
amongst the Yoruba, who were the majority of inner city residents.

Traditionally, when a girl married into a Yoruba family, she
took her place in a hierarchy of status, assuming rights and
duties, not only towards her husband, but his whole family.
She called his seniors 'father' or 'mother', and his juniors 'husband'—since, if he died, to one of them would fall the responsibility of taking her as wife. As a bride, she was inducted into
the crucial institution of society, the patrilineage: she lived in
its compound, subject to the authority of its head, and deferred
to her seniors. (See Lloyd, 1955 and Schwab, 1958.) Her
conduct was important to them all, for the future of the line
depended on the children she bore them. The marriage was
protected by a pledge between the two families it joined—the
bridewealth paid by the husband and his kin. If the marriage
failed from the wife's fault—if she proved barren, or ran away,
or misbehaved intolerably—her family were obliged to return
the valuable presents they had received; while if she left her
husband for good reasons, his family could not reclaim them.
Either way, the failure was expensive to one family or the
other—wealth had been laid out for nothing, or returned when
it was needed to provide the wife's brothers with the means to
marry. Both families, therefore, had a direct interest in ensur-
ing that the couple treated each other fairly.

Despite the emphasis upon the patrilineage, a wife retained
rights within her parents' family. If need be, at least in the
Southern Yoruba cities, she could claim upon their land and
property for herself and her children. For both men and
women, their economic security, political status and social
identity were determined, not by any single relationship, but by
their membership in kin groups as a whole. Marriage defined
where children belonged, but the relationship between husband

and wife was not itself, I think, expected to express any particular intimacy or intensity of emotional loyalty, especially since a man might have several wives. In Lagos, if men and women idealised any sentimental attachment, or expressed a predominant personal loyalty, it was above all to their mothers, and sometimes to a brother or sister of the same mother close to them in age. Beyond the immediate household, the kin group as a whole commanded the over-riding loyalty. Marriage was not expected to express a diffuse emotional commitment, or prove, in an isolated relationship, a sense of belonging and fulfilment.

This tradition rested upon the stability of tangible economic assets—the family compound, with its many rooms arranged about a courtyard, which guaranteed shelter; the family land, which guaranteed a livelihood and an inheritance for its children; the bridewealth, which guaranteed collective responsibility for marital conduct. None of these held the same power of sanction in an urban money economy, where people mostly rented accommodation and worked for a wage. Rights in land or a family house in another town were of little use to a trader, clerk or labourer. Even the bridewealth, translated into money, became a less trustworthy pledge, since cash already spent is harder to reclaim than goods. But the improvisations by which marriage adapted to these circumstances only gradually changed its nature.

Though the family no longer controlled so exclusively the means of earning a living, it still provided most people with their only security. If they fell sick, lost their jobs, were retired, or if they needed money to pay their children's school fees or to retrieve a failing trade, the family was the one resource to which everyone could appeal. Some long-established Lagos families maintained a house which remained the headquarters of its affairs: elderly relatives found shelter in its rambling courtyards, the head of the family and some of his married sons occupied the principal rooms, and the family councils were held there. But families which owned no property settled in rented rooms in the same compact neighbourhood, exchanging daily visits. Everyone had family affairs continually in mind, and in the cool of the evening would make the rounds, passing news, discussing problems, bringing a present of food for an elderly aunt or a shilling for a favourite nephew. The family would meet more formally once a week, or once a month, to review the needs of its members and arrange how to meet them. Money would be raised, according to the means of each, to pay a doctor, educate a child, support someone out of work; the family network would look out for a job for a new-comer or find him a place to stay; disputes would be arbitrated. Few people had such secure and well-paid posts that they could afford to neglect this system of mutual support, and these few held such authority in it, and contributed so much, that they could not honourably withdraw.

Thus the collective solidarity of kinsfolk remained the crucial insurance against hardship. But it no longer offered much protection to a marriage. The bridewealth had become a trivial sum, compared with the expenses of a proper wedding, and a man might find it from his own savings. Few bothered to reclaim it if their wives left them, and some parents no longer asked it, preferring the money to be spent on their daughter's welfare. More and more men found their own wives, and married without any formal arrangement between the families, even without asking their parents' consent. A wife who lived with her husband in a rented room, and did not claim on their property, who cost them nothing and whom they had not chosen, was not of much concern to his kinsmen, though her children would be. She could no longer be sure that if she complained to her husband's family, her case would be fairly listened to in his family councils. She depended more than in the past on her own parents, brothers and sisters. And since the patrilineage no longer determined the allocation of crucial economic resources, she had less reason to throw in her lot with her husband's family, and become its loyal daughter.

Marriage, therefore, was not now an alliance between two families, but between a man and a woman whose most compelling loyalties were still to the families in which they were born. It could provide a woman with only fragile security. Her husband might fall sick, lose his job, desert her for another wife, and in these misfortunes the goodwill of his family was uncertain—especially if the match was not of their making. As an insurance against such risks, and to contribute to the needs of her own kinsfolk, she wanted an income of her own. So it

became a custom in Lagos, as part of the marriage agreement
between a couple, for a husband to provide his wife, as best he
could, with money to capitalise a petty trade, to learn typing or
dressmaking, or set up a shop. She was not expected to contribute these earnings to the household expenses: and if she sometimes did so when her husband was in want, he acknowledged
her generosity. This independent source of income became a
crucial counter-weight to the shifting bias of vulnerability.

Women had traded in Yoruba society in the past, and
married women had always retained customary rights in their
father's lineage. But these aspects of tradition acquired a new
emphasis, as they came to substitute for other, outdated safe-
guards against mistreatment in marriage. Kinship adjusted
by a more even balance between the claims of a man and
woman's lineage. Trade or job became a more central preoccupation of women: if they were forced to choose between
their husband and their economic interest, their own earnings
often promised a more dependable support. Marriage was a
contract of limited obligations: to bear a man children and
keep his house; to pay the housekeeping allowance and finance
a woman's livelihood. But it was a contract between two people, largely unprotected by the concern or authority of their
kin. The wife's obligations to her kinsfolk and her occupation
now competed with her husband's claims. The success of the
marriage relied on mutual respect for the independence each
partner needed to retain.

The pattern was, perhaps, inherently unstable. The principle
of collective security had survived, but it no longer rested on
collective control of economic assets. It drew on subscription
of wages and profits individually earned, and so the immediate
interest of each member of the family was less functionally integrated with the welfare of his kin. The interdependence of
marriage, kinship and means of livelihood disintegrated under
the pressures of an urban money economy into an uneasy
equilibrium between potentially incompatible interests. But
the meaning of each relationship had not essentially changed.
Marriage was still subordinate to kinship. The celebrations of
the lineage—when a hundred or more relatives forgathered,
handsomely dressed in festival uniforms, to know and renew
their ties to each other—still symbolised the most fundamental

attachment of life. The mutual solidarity of kin was still, for
most people, their essential security and the crucial definition
of their social identity. This continuity with the past enabled
people still to base their expectations of each other on traditional values. The uncertainties of married life in the city were
manageable, because the situations which might arise could be
understood by everyone in the same terms. Though marriage
was probably more threatened by competing loyalties than in
the past, the risks were predictable, and the purposes
unchanged. A couple knew what constituted provocation or
reprisal in marital conflict, how to avoid or exploit it, and what
the response should be. They might be vulnerable but for better or worse they knew where they stood.

The streets of central Lagos reflected this pattern of life. The
narrow alleys were crowded with women hawking their wares
—bolts of cloth, cola nuts, cigarettes, tins of groceries—
gracefully balanced in baskets on their heads; grandmothers
traded from their doorsteps, as much to be part of the life of
the street as to sell their few dusty articles; dressmakers bent
over sewing machines on the porches of the houses; cooks
tossed fried cakes over charcoal braziers for the clerks from
the city offices. All day and late into the evening people passed
to and fro to work, to the great markets which surrounded the
neighbourhood, to negotiate a business deal or visit relatives
and friends. The houses huddled together in an irregular mo-
saic of courtyards and passages, their dark and overcrowded
rooms opening onto spaces where women cooked and washed,
children played, men talked. Some rooms would be occupied
by the members of a lineage, whose head, perhaps, conducted
his business from the front parlour; others were rented out.
For tenants and owners alike, their family connections
branched through the neighbouring streets, so that as they
came home from work, or school or market, they called on
grandparents, aunts, parents, brothers and sisters, cousins, exchanging greetings, making small gifts to the elderly, passing
news. By the layout of its dwellings, designed not for a single
household but a group of related households; by the intermingling of domestic life and petty trade; by the compactness
of the clusters of family networks; by the indifference to the
amenity of the cramped and sparsely furnished rooms, which

provided parents and children with their only intimate private space; by the gregariousness of its streets, central Lagos expressed faithfully the values and meanings of the lives it sheltered.

THE REHOUSING ESTATE

The rehousing estate embodied, just as explicitly, a profoundly different conception of life—a cut-price translation of English suburban homeliness. The neat terraced cottages were designed for a single household: kitchen, living room, bedroom leading off each other in an integrated pattern which two families could not suitably share. Street trading was forbidden, and besides, the roads were empty and lifeless, as people dispersed to the city for the day. Commerce was segregated in a shopping centre. The nearest places of employment were several miles away. Instinctively perhaps, as much as purposefully, the planners built into the estate all the conventional expectations of an English middle class: the domestic intimacy of a married couple and their brood, house-proud and autonomous; the segregation of a residential neighbourhood amongst greenery and fresh air, in peaceful retreat from work and commerce; the concern for privacy, cleanliness and the orderly separation of functions, each to its designated space. It could hardly have been less adaptable to the dominant lifestyle of the evicted residents of Lagos whom it was designed to rehabilitate.

Even if the amenities of a suburban home had appealed to them, they could not afford the cost in fares, the rent of space, the higher price of food in local shops. Craftsmen and traders lacked the resources to capitalise a modern workshop or grocery store, and survive months of poor business in the hope of creating a market: most went bankrupt, or returned to the city. Life on the estate imposed a reallocation of resources from the claims of kinsfolk, now scattered and less obtrusive, to the maintenance of a private household in dignified surroundings. And this symbolic emphasis on marriage, as the relationship above all to be enhanced and protected, adorned with shrubs and flowers and polished furniture, was not only beyond the means of most people, but meaningless. Their

ideals and the most important rituals of everyday life were embodied in other relationships. They could understand the value
of less cramped quarters and more solid building, but these
amenities were trivial compared with the sacrifices they en-
tailed. Old people became isolated, their needs unnoticed: a
nephew who could afford to give his aunt sixpence could not so
readily spend twice as much to ride the bus to visit her. Family
councils lapsed as their members dispersed, some driven from
the estate by its costs, others preferring from the first to find
room in more familiar parts of the city. The people of central
Lagos were unused to the means by which social contacts are
maintained across a distance—letters, telephone calls, visiting
by appointment, tracing addresses from street names and
numbers, the ordering of time to complement the segregated
ordering of spaces. Thus they possessed neither the money, nor
the habitual skills, nor the sense of life's meaning which the estate implied. It robbed them of the physical support for an
identity they could not afford to relinquish. Those who
remained on the estate could only struggle against its hardships
and inconveniences, in the hope that their resistance would
sooner or later break the alien rigidity of its pattern.
Meanwhile they were still, when I talked with them, mourning
the loss of their old homes.

Yet the planners of the estate recognised, at least intuitively,
a latent contradiction in Lagos society, which the pattern of
life in the city centre could not altogether resolve. Kinship did
not control economic opportunities or receive their rewards,
however much it struggled to secure them for the benefit of the
family as a whole. Whatever the obligation to repay kinsfolk
for the scholarship they had subscribed, or the position won
through their influence, the advantages were formally personal. The ablest and most fortunate were no longer dependent
on the solidarity of the lineage. Family loyalties continually
claimed upon them, sometimes exorbitantly, but secure in permanent, pensionable, salaried posts, they had no reciprocal
demands to make. Their children's future would be determined, not by the rights of lineage, but educational qualifications: and the more they restricted the scope of their obligations to kin, the more readily they could pay for good schools
and study overseas. A new middle class was emerging, for

whom the inherited loyalties of kinship contradicted their economic interest, so long as both rich and poor remained one
family. The physical structure of the old city disguised this
class distinction: the rambling family houses, with their dark,
shabby rooms, had nowhere to display personal wealth, while
the claims of kinship obtruded everywhere. At home, it was
hard to tell a rich merchant from a labourer: both wore the
same singlet and frayed khaki shorts, sat on the same wooden
stools, and slept on the same bed of hard cords. Wealth showed
in open handed hospitality and authority in the family councils. Many of the younger men, especially, struggling to secure
their middle class status, felt trapped by these pressures. Support for relatives ran them into debt, their children's education
was still to pay for, and they had begun to see, through the
eyes of their European colleagues, a disreputable, backward
squalor in their surroundings.

The rehousing estate catered to these discontents. It embodied the aspirations of the socially ambitious, and helped to
defend them. Here a young clerk could furnish a parlour with
a bookshelf and radio and study his correspondence courses in
peace, secure that dunning relatives would seldom find him.
His wife could serve tea and biscuits like a proper English
lady, and keep the children at their homework. To the estate's
planner, this was the intelligible pattern of progress, and they
set out to serve it. They were not insensitive to the hardships of
rehousing, and would have liked to relieve them. The director
of the Lagos Executive Development Board was not surprised
or unconcerned at the distress described in the report I
presented to him. But he could not compromise the underlying
conception without, in his own eyes, discrediting the meaning
of his work. He insisted that any remedies must first accept the
basic premise of the scheme. The essential purpose was not the
replacement of dilapidated, insanitary, overcrowded houses,
but the reformation of a way of life. Articulate public opinion
supported him. Educated Nigerians who, if they had consulted
their own experience, might have seen a different reality, endorsed the same conventional interpretation of progress. Central Lagos was an anomaly, mocking the image of the modern
capital whose concrete office blocks were thrusting above its
rusty tin roofs. The rehousing estate, at least as a symbol of in-

tent, was designed to resolve the ambiguity inherent in the city's structure, to expose the latent divergencies of interest and establish to whom the future belonged.

The director of the Lagos scheme was an engineer by training, and he saw its difficulties as problems of social engineering to which a solution must exist. To abandon the scheme would be as much a failure of professional resourcefulness, he told me, as for a civil engineer, commissioned to design a bridge, to confess himself beaten by the awkwardness of the terrain. A few years later, talking with his counterpart in Boston, I met the same passionate professional commitment to solving social problems by physical means, the same sense of betrayal when the validity of these means was challenged. Both men had accepted the task of changing society by changing its buildings, and the clearer it became that changes could not be accomplished in this way, the more they were driven to self-deception and counter-accusations to protect their identity as sincere reformers. Their personal predicament reflected a fundamental drawback of all idealistic slum clearance schemes.

Physical squalor is an affront to the order of society, which readily becomes associated with other signs of disorder in the public image. Crime, drunkenness, prostitution, feckless poverty, mental pathology do indeed cluster where housing is poorest—though not there only. Once this association has been taken for granted, any anomalous pattern of life embodied in shabby surroundings is easily assumed to be pathological, without much regard for the evidence. Bad housing thus becomes a symbol of complex discordances in the structure of society and so to be treated as if it were a cause of them. In this way, society hands its most intractable problems to professional administrators, who accept the ideals which underlie their assignment, but are neither trained nor required to search out the social implications. The Lagos Executive Development Board must have been vaguely aware of the nature of marriage in the city, and the importance of petty trading to it. They knew the tradition of kinship, and the part it played in social insurance. But they were not obliged to work out how these patterns of relationship inhered in the old city, reinforcing and complementing each other, and confront the implications.

Their practical task was constrained by more urgent considerations of land prices, subsidies, rent income, building costs, time-tables and political pressures. Just as the social problem had been identified with squalid housing, so the solution became identified with housing of another kind—and the more spectacular the physical contrast, the more impressive the image of reform.

SLUMS AS SOCIAL SYMBOLS

The Lagos experience must, I believe, be repeated whenever slum clearance is confused with broader ambitions of social reform. And it is in such situations that it characteristically provokes reactions akin to bereavement, for it is then that it threatens the sense of identity and most frustrates the search for a manageable continuity in the interpretation of relationships.

When people are forced to move from a familiar neighbourhood, they lose, most obviously, the habitual physical setting of their lives. To the planners who move them, this setting has an unambiguous meaning. It is a slum—dirty, dilapidated, overcrowded and dangerous to health. The signs of dirt and decay can be powerfully persuasive. When I escorted visiting friends from England around the alleys of old Lagos, they were too shocked by the ordure floating in the muddy rivulets over which they had to pick their way, by the dark rooms with stained and patched walls, by the jostle of livestock and naked children, to listen when I insisted that the area was not, by the standards of Nigeria then, either particularly poor or unhealthy. It was full of prosperous families, had a flourishing trade, and was close by the best medical services in the country. Dirt is laden with connotations of danger and corruption once it is perceived as something anomalous and disordered (see Douglas, 1966). But the lives of people in slums are not necessarily disorderly, and so they may not notice the dirt, or see it only as an incidental nuisance. They would like more space, better drains, repairs—but to achieve this only at the cost of destroying the neighbourhood itself seems to them an inconceivable distortion of what is important. If the physical setting has one meaning to the planning authority, it has another to the residents. The corner shops, the shabby streets, the yards and lots where they played as children are invested with all kinds of intimate associations. They identify with the neighbourhood: it is part of them, and to hear it condemned as a slum is a condemnation of themselves too.

The condemnation may be explicitly personal. To the authorities, decay and obsolescence suggest economic backwardness and poverty. The physical symbols are so evocative of social disorder, a critical analysis of the association between them seems pedantic or even subversive. Hence, if the residents cling to their slum, they too must be, at best, appallingly ignorant of the possibilities of life, and at worst morally corrupt. Slum clearance acquires a missionary zeal. Robert Weaver, Administrator of the United States Housing and Home Finance Agency when, a few years later, it was still promoting urban renewal projects like the West End of Boston, urged enthusiastically, 'It is just at the moment that a family has been uprooted, has been provided through relocation assistance with the means of establishing a new home, and has been brought into contact . . . with the social agencies of the community, that miracles can be accomplished.'[1] In Nigeria, the Minister of Lagos Affairs described the slum area as 'a humiliation to any person with a sense of national pride'; and the principal daily newspaper commented censoriously, when the residents attempted to defend themselves against eviction (*Daily Times,* Lagos, 30 June 1956):

> The spectacle was saddening, and it was bound to arouse the anger of every lover of Nigeria and those who rightly feel that Lagos should, and can, be a worthier capital. It should have occurred to the occupants, and their leaders in particular, that by indulging in foolhardiness, they had only themselves to blame if the police, with Nigeria behind them, got the better of them.

[1] To be fair, Robert Weaver himself has written much more critically of the problems of urban renewal. See for instance his paper 'Major factors in urban planning' (1963). But here I am concerned with the way renewal was presented, officially, as public policy.

Thus in both the West End of Boston and central Lagos, clearance involved a conflict between incompatible conceptions of the place itself. The residents and the redevelopment authorities had different interests, and valued the amenities of life with a different emphasis, but they also saw the neighbourhood in quite different terms. Each had learned to attach a meaning to it which the other could not understand. To one it was an anomaly, to the other an integral part of their lives. Neither could revise their conception without radically reconstructing the assumptions on which their purposes and expectations were based. If central Lagos was not a slum, then all kinds of beliefs about modernisation and nationhood were invalidated: and if it was, then the people who lived there were betraying the aspirations of their country by insisting on their right to be themselves. The redevelopment authority could not allow itself to see that it was destroying anything of value, and it tried to rehouse the evicted families in a physical setting which repudiated all the characteristic features of the old. To defend the consistency of its own conception of society, it had to deny any continuity in the experience of those it expropriated. In this sense, it was just as conservative in its attachment to conventional notions of modernity as the residents were in clinging to their old homes. In much the same spirit, the redevelopment of the West End set out to rebuild a conventional middle-class community in the city centre and, by dislodging its immigrant Italian residents, hustle them along the traditional way to assimilation.

The merging of social reform in slum clearance, therefore, attaches a meaning to particular streets and houses wider than their amenity or discomfort, or the memories they recall. The definition of a slum is also a definition of the people who live there. Their own attachment to the neighbourhood is reinforced by the insistence of authority that in moving they must change, not merely their surroundings, but the way they live. A situation is created which resembles bereavement in the sudden and irretrievable nature of the loss, yet provides no process akin to mourning, by which the loss can be assimilated and the essential continuity of life restored. Like death, the moment of transition is abrupt: the household wakes one morning in familiar surroundings and by nightfall is gone for ever. And as in

grieving for the dead, all the purposes and understanding inherent in those surroundings have to be retrieved and
refashioned so that they still make sense of life elsewhere. If
the new home is adaptable to their way of life, the adjustment
is soon made—the same conventions of neighbourliness apply,
the old patterns of shopping, meeting, visiting find their counterpart in new spaces. The predictability of the new environment is not hard to learn, since it involves no radical revision
of the past. But when social ideals are invested in slum clearance, such a comfortable transition is ruled out.

In Robert Weaver's words, what is to be accomplished is not
the recreation of a way of life, without rats, dirt and
overcrowding, but a miracle—a shock of enlightenment which,
like a religious conversion, transforms a person overnight. Any
restoration of a familiar pattern of relationships is deliberately
frustrated: and since people cannot assimilate change without
continuity, they are bound to evade the purposes of slum clearance in any way they can. The outcome can be destructive, not
only for the residents without resources to defend themselves,
but for society at large, which finds its ideals committed to
issues for which there is no humane resolution and in which it
can only fail.

I have tried to show how slum clearance can be a form of
bereavement. Eviction from the neighbourhood in which one
was at home can be almost as disruptive of the meaning of life
as the loss of a crucial relationship. Dispossession threatens the
whole structure of attachments through which purposes are
embodied, because these attachments cannot readily be re-
established in an alien setting. In this slum clearance represents the implications of any change where people are dispossessed of the familiar context of their lives, though the loss
may be less sudden and the object of attachment less tangible.
In all such situations, the ambivalence of grieving has to work
itself out.

But if slum clearance illustrates how social changes can
provoke grief, it constrains the outcome more than most. This,
as we have seen, is its peculiar insensitivity. The abrupt transition to a new housing estate pre-empts the tentative adjustments by which a widow or a widower, for instance, can act
out their conflicting responses to loss. These, too, have their

counterparts in social changes. The ambivalence of loss can become embodied in intermediate forms of adjustment which, like a period of mourning, hold the resolution of the conflict in suspense. The dynamic of grieving is then projected into these collective reactions, which bear the same hope of leading towards a reintegration, and the same risk of morbid irresolution as individual grief. This is the theme of the next chapter.

IV
TRIBALISM

So far we have considered two situations where a familiar pattern of relationships is so suddenly and radically disrupted that the ability to make sense of life may for a while be overwhelmed by despair. In bereavement, the slow and painful process of recovery is supported, if only residually, by mourning customs. But the slum clearance schemes did not allow for any process of transition, and the hardship they caused was therefore much harder to overcome, frustrating their intentions as instruments of social policy.

I turn now to an example of institutions which do seem to articulate such a process—tribal associations in Nigeria. They arose in response to the same confusions and emerging class distinctions of city life which influenced the Lagos clearance scheme. But where slum clearance committed policy to a single-minded conception of social evolution, they sought to mediate more ambivalently between town and country, tradition and modernity, working out a gradual reconciliation. Nor were the pioneers of tribal associations as hostile to change as most of the residents of central Lagos, though they mourned the disintegration of their traditions. The example shows how a sense of loss may arise from changes in society which people partly accept; and how the ambivalence of this acceptance is reflected in institutions which articulate conflicts analogous to the impulses of grief. The personal confusion of identity, provoked by the disruption of cultures and communities, becomes displaced onto collective expressions of a common dilemma.

Let me call this collective response tribalism, since the assertion of tribal identities in a modern African state is one of its most obvious illustrations. But any search to express a group identity, where people have lost their bearings in a heterogeneous society, falls within my definition. Later in the chapter, for instance, I discuss the experience of university students and ethnic minorities in the same terms. In all these situations, I believe, an ambivalence fundamentally similar to grieving is working itself out: and the process is as vulnerable to abortive outcomes as personal grief. Tribalism expresses a dilemma which cannot well be ignored. Yet it contains dangerous impulses of retreat and rejection which continually threaten to break out. The examples which follow illustrate the way tribalism articulates a sense of loss, and how it may be overwhelmed by the forces it seeks to balance.

Listen, for instance, to the opening remarks of the chairman of a meeting called to inaugurate a tribal association in Eastern Nigeria in 1942. His speech expresses the ambivalent ideals of such associations—at once a lament for a tradition betrayed, and a justification of change. This ambivalence is represented, too, in the circumstances of the meeting. For though the aim was to retrieve the virtues and loyalties of the past, the speaker was himself a pioneer of change, and he spoke, not to those who had remained faithful to village life, but to those who had followed him in search of opportunities in the new colonial cities. Though the audience was all from the same group of villages (which he calls a 'town'), they lived and worked in Enugu, the administrative headquarters of the region where the meeting was held. As his son remembers, the chairman said:

'There was a time when no one from our town lived in Enugu. But gradually our numbers increased and today we are many. Here we are, for no other purpose than to find our daily bread. This does not imply that we did not live well in our old homes. . . . In our villages we enjoyed a full life. And if the white man had not come, we could have continued with our happy village life. . . . The white man came with education and civilisation, and our ideas and outlook changed. Even within the village we behaved in a different way. It was this change of outlook that gave us the courage to leave the village. We have no reason to blame ourselves for taking this course, for we know how much we have benefited financially and educationally.

'But I would like you to consider this question. Are our
villages the same as they were before the white man came?
Emphatically no! Even before we left the village we were
aware of certain changes. Indeed, some of us were responsible for a number of these changes. But what we did was not
harmful. Other changes—constant litigation, frequent quarrels, bribery and corruption—things completely foreign to
our village—were the result of the machinations of a certain
unpopular group of our people.

'My fellow citizens, it is just a few decades since we came
under the influence of Western Civilisation. If, within this
short period, chaos has invaded the village to such an extent, what can we expect for the future? If we sit with our
hands folded and let matters get worse, what will be the
verdict of our children, the leaders of tomorrow? They will
find reconstruction even more difficult because they know
less than we do about the village past. . . . Though I re-
frained in the past from taking part in village ceremonies,
many of which are now dying out, I am beginning to feel
that there was something valuable in certain of the ceremonies and that they should be revived and conserved.

'This union has two main objectives—to seek the interest
of its members, and to seek the welfare of our town. . . .
Let us look back to the days of our illustrious ancestors, by
dint of whose labour we enjoyed a happy village life. Today
we are proud of them. What will the coming generations say
of us? We can earn their approval if only we do something
to make them say with pride, "This is my town, these are my
customs, here I belong."' (Okafor Omali, 1965, pp.
139–41.)

The speech expresses eloquently the interplay of conservatism and innovation in the founding of the association. It
makes no apology for promoting change. Indeed, the association itself is to be an innovation, and with its written constitution and formal procedures, draws on British rather than Ibo
conventions. But the appeal is to tradition, to a reintegration of
society through its past. At the same time, although the
problems presented are those of the village—the corruption of
the warrant chiefs, litigation, the decay of custom—the initiative for the association comes, not from the stay-at-homes, but
from the migrants who have settled in the modern cities. The
speaker himself, in his own career, had experienced the same

conflicting impulses. As a child he had defied his mother's anger and the dismay of his age mates to go to school, cultivating tabooed bush land to pay his fees. He was the first from his village to complete six years of missionary education, the first to travel beyond the neighbouring settlements, to see Lagos and live amongst people of another tribe. He brought up his son to speak English before his native language. But he also became the initiator of the movement to recall the wanderers to their homeland, and restore the customs he had repudiated in his youth.

Within a few years, the association he founded—the Enugu-Ukwu Patriotic Union—had branches in Lagos and Northern Nigeria, besides most of the major townships of the East. Altogether there were seventy-seven chapters, organised in eight groups, all co-ordinated through the central headquarters in Enugu. The association assumed in time four principal functions. First, it tackled the corruption and endless litigation into which village affairs had degenerated: it secured the right to nominate representatives to the Appeal Court of the native system of justice, laying down by-laws to regulate their conduct; it overthrew the corrupt warrant chiefs; and it forbade any member of the village to take his fellow-countryman to court, insisting that all disputes be settled by the Union itself. Second, it sought to reintegrate the townsmen with village society by instituting a General Return Home every three years, when everyone was required to foregather in the village with their families, from all over Nigeria, or pay a heavy fine. Third, it drew subscriptions from its wage-earning members in the towns to finance village improvements—an extension to the market, a post office, a cottage hospital—and acted as a lobby for government grants. Last, the local branches looked after the welfare of the urban migrants, helping newcomers to find jobs and a place to stay, repatriating the sick or daughters who disgraced the village by prostitution, providing for funeral expenses and cases of hardship. Thus although the association saw itself as reviving the traditions of the village council, its aims were progressive, and it dealt with the urgent problems of contemporary life. Descriptions of other Ibo associations give a similar account of their functions:

Ethnic associations perform 'urban roles'; they give assistance in litigation, illness and death (return of corpse to
home place, repatriation of family); they are a channel of
information on urban conditions, in particular employment
opportunities; they act as arbitrators between members; in
special circumstances they may even provide educational fa-
cilities in town. Thus the Ibo Northern Region Union ran
two primary and two secondary schools in Northern
Nigeria. The main concern of these associations is, however,
with the affairs of the home community. In Eastern Nigeria
decisions on village affairs are taken not so much by the
village residents as by co-villagers living in towns. If many
an association calls itself 'Improvement Union' this refers to
the improvement not of urban living conditions but of the
home area represented by the association. They transmit
new ideas and aspirations, they constitute an urban lobby
for village interests, they counsel on village developments,
but above all they finance the major of such developments;
the building of roads and bridges, schools, hospitals or water
supply systems; they offer scholarships, at times with the
specific object of providing local staff for the institutions
they are establishing. In some villages an institution called
'Mass Rally' has come into existence. This practice was
probably started in 'Furnace Town' . . . mass returns to the
home village on a specific date have been organised in other
places recently. The regular intervals between these meet-
ings vary from two to five years. They usually take place at
Christmas time. (Gugler, 1970, pp. 29–30.)

These local patriotic unions helped to articulate an evolving
national society. They linked town and country, taxing the
prosperity of the developing urban economy to improve the
village, and they provided a supportive community for the
townsman, protecting him from insecurity and guiding him
through the unfamiliar complexity of city life. Their political
counterpart was a conception of federalism which would both
ensure the political unity of Nigeria and respect its diversity of
language and culture. Thus the National Council of Nigeria
and the Cameroons, which became a predominantly Ibo party
with its majority support in the Eastern Region, campaigned
under the slogan 'One Nigeria' and consistently opposed
Northern threats of secession. At the same time, it exploited

the Ibo associations as a means of mobilising party support. Politically and socially, the organisations which evolved continually tried to balance the claims of national and local interests, at once tribal and universal in their principles.

Like a process of mourning, therefore, the response to the passing of traditional society was characteristically ambivalent, caught between nostalgia for the past, and a desire to pre-empt the future by establishing all at once the ideal of a united nation. But like mourning, tribalism as a principle of accommodation could also be abortive if the conflict inherent in the process became unmanageable. Grief may become petrified in a posture of misery or ritual lament; it may be suppressed in a bustle of superficial, practical activity; or displaced into neurotic symptoms. Each of these responses tries to evade the conflict, either by denying it altogether, or by exaggerating one of its opposing impulses at the expense of the other. So, too, in the evolution of Ibo affairs, the ability to contain the conflict and postpone a premature resolution of the issues of tribal and national identification was continually at risk. It was vulnerable to impulses both of outright secession and impatient unification, to moods of despair and outbursts of hatred, as the frustrations became unbearable.

Despite their adaptability, the Ibo were, I think, always peculiarly liable to see themselves as victims, whose sufferings marked them out, like the children of Israel, for a tragic destiny. In a presidential address to the Ibo State Assembly in 1949, Dr Nnamdi Azikiwe gave these feelings a characteristic rhetorical flourish: 'It would appear that God has specially created the Ibo people to suffer persecution and to be victimised because of their resolute will to live. Since suffering is the label of our tribe, we can afford to be sacrificed for the ultimate redemption of the children of Africa.' The whole speech is a catalogue of Ibo greatness and Ibo wrongs, and in later speeches before similar audiences, the same theme recurs: the Ibo had been singled out for persecution, because of their indomitable pride in their cultural heritage, and their destiny as leaders of Nigeria. This tendency to define identity in terms of suffering, to make a virtue of a tragic role, recalls the posture of chronic grief. In the writings of Ibo novelists, too, the conflict between tradition and modernity is handled with a more despairing sense of loss, a purer ennobling of an idealised past than in the work of other African authors. I do not want to exaggerate a mood which appears only here and there in the expression of Ibo self-consciousness. But the confidence, even arrogance, of Ibo assertion seems from the first to have been shadowed by underlying grief; and when finally the Ibo broke with the Federation, this readiness to cast themselves in a tragic role may, I believe, have strengthened their commitment to desperate remedies.

Yet the Ibo were also the most consistent advocates of Nigerian unity. Their dispersal in search of opportunities outside their homeland, to which local patriotism and tribal self-consciousness was a reaction, also gave them a particular interest in securing the economic integration of Nigeria. They needed, especially, to protect their position in the Northern cities, where they had established prosperous communities, but remained socially isolated in the strangers' quarters. Hence their nationalism was bound up with tribal self-interest, and provoked a reactive tribalism amongst people with less stake in the unity of the federation.

The Ibo associations were more widespread and coherently organised than those of other Nigerian peoples, because over-population drove more of them to seek employment outside their homeland. The Yoruba, in the more prosperous and less crowded Western Region, had less incentive to migrate beyond their traditional boundaries: while the Northerners, though their region was poor, lacked the education to exploit the opportunities even in their own cities. Perhaps, too, the Ibo had a greater need to create new institutions to express their identity, since unlike the Yoruba and Hausa they had no history of political hegemony to which to refer their tribal self-consciousness. But as soon as the Ibo intruded upon the territory of others, these too were exposed to the threat of cultural dispossession. In the North, especially, the Ibo represented the disruptive forces of change—an alien invasion, besieging the old cities from the settlements beneath their crumbling walls. Tribalism provoked tribalism, as Northerners saw a mutually supportive community of strangers extending its hold over commerce and employment. Tribal self-consciousness was partly a reaction against the tribalism of others, defined as much by repudiating alien ways as by asserting one's own. And when people draw the boundaries of where they do not belong, their insecurity will project upon those they exclude menacing and disparaging qualities.

Within a group, tribal associations express the need to reconcile cultural continuity with a relevant strategy for dealing with modern life. Externally, they represent a parallel dilemma: how to identify with the nation without being overwhelmed by strangers, who may rob you not only of your livelihood but of a sense of your own being. Hence the tribal boundaries which protect the integrity of each group are sensitive to any disturbance of this delicate balance. Once upset, the hostility towards others latent in tribal self-consciousness breaks out in violent denunciation. The more secure a tribal group, the more confident of its collective identity, the less fear will be projected upon its stereotypes of other tribes. It views outsiders patronisingly, even with ridicule or scorn, but without hatred. Yet its very self-confidence may make it insensitive to the threat it presents. It treats the hostility it provokes as no more dangerous than its own chauvinism, blind to the intensity of hatred swelling towards a paranoid outburst.

So long as Nigeria was governed by an uneasy alliance of regionally based parties, the Ibo tried to reconcile regional autonomy and universal rights of citizenship within the framework of the federal constitution. But the civilian government collapsed in January 1966. After this first *coup d'état,* Ibo civil servants came to dominate the policy of central government under the leadership of an Ibo general. They saw an opportunity to resolve the tensions of federalism by promulgating a unitary state. A united civil service, a more centralised political structure and an open economic system would all have favoured Ibo enterprise. But such a solution ignored the underlying anxieties which federalism tried to contain. It triggered the latent violence implicit in the tribal stereotypes, whose seriousness had never been appreciated by the Ibo leaders.

In May, when General Ironsi announced the unification of the civil service, the first massacre of Ibos took place in Northern cities. It was followed by a second in July, after the second *coup,* and a third in September, of horrifying atrocity. Thousands were killed, and the refugees fled to their homeland 'hacked, slashed, mangled, stripped naked and robbed of all their possessions. . . . Men, women and children arrived with arms and legs broken, hands hacked off, mouths split open. Pregnant women were cut open and their unborn children killed.' Though the massacres were politically instigated, and carefully planned, the cruelty of their execution seemed to exceed even the bitterest of political conflicts. Over the years, Northern perception of the Ibo had been manipulated and distorted into a stereotype which was scarcely human. Reporting on the massacres, Colin Legum drew attention to the influence of this propaganda (1966):

> Last year I visited the North and was disturbed by the intensity of anti-Ibo feeling. While the peasants complained of exploitation, the educated Northerners spoke of the Ibo as vermin, criminals, money-grabbers, and sub-humans without genuine culture. 'Their god is money,' they said. This de-humanising process struck me as alarming, but the Ibo leaders criticised my warnings as merely reflecting feudal Hausa sentiments.

He concluded that besides the fear of Ibo domination, and the internal tensions of Northern society, the vilification of the Ibo was an essential factor in the massacres. This perversion of conflict into irrational hatred embodied, not only jealousy of Ibo prosperity, but an hysterical defence of tribal integrity, in which the disparaging stereotyping of another tribe came to justify outright brutality. It lowered the inhibitions against harming other human beings, by vilifying them in sub-human terms.

I do not mean to imply an exact equivalence between the evolution of these tragic events and the progress of grief. Nor do the dilemmas of tribalism themselves explain why the massacres should have led to civil war, despite attempts to renegotiate the federation. But the analogies between grieving and the complex of responses which give rise to tribalism seem to me so close that they can be understood as varieties of the same fundamental process. Both arise from situations where the

meaningfulness of life is threatened by the loss of familiar relationships. Like the bereaved, an African villager can hardly
make sense of events around him, because the context of purpose by which he used to interpret them has been undermined.
What do wealth, status, marriage, honour mean in a society
where traditional, colonial and autonomous national institutions overlay each other in such rapid succession that the values and symbols of three different periods of history, each
derived from a different framework of assumptions, are
present all at once? The loss of meaning is not as abrupt and
overwhelming as in bereavement, but it is cumulative, as the
implications of the creation of nation states work themselves
out. And though he is not so traumatically robbed of the relationships which embody his purposes, an African villager,
unlike the bereaved, has to cope with an increasingly unfamiliar social environment, as strangers intrude into village life, or
he settles in towns where the principles of interaction between
people of different tribes all have to be discovered. The ability
to interpret events, and predict from experience the outcome
of behaviour, is doubly threatened: he is less sure of what he
wants, and less sure how others will react to him and how he
should respond so as to secure what he wants. In these circumstances, he is caught between the same conflicting impulses as
the bereaved: to return to the past, which seems in retrospect a
haven of security and meaningful satisfactions; or to realise at
once a new self, a modern man confidently handling the possibilities of a progressive nation. Each impulse provokes its painful reaction: the attempt to revive tradition only exposes its
decay; the pursuit of modernity leads to humiliating frustrations and bewilderment, and a sense of betrayal of his true
identity. The conflict cannot be evaded or resolved, but only
worked out through a long process of reinterpretation, by
which the essential understanding of life, embedded in the experience of each tribe, is abstracted from its traditional context
and reformulated.

This process finds its intellectual expression in concepts of
negritude, African personality, African socialism, which seek
to graft contemporary political ideology on to indigenous
roots; in anthropological studies like Jomo Kenyatta's *Facing
Mount Kenya* which, conversely, interpret traditional institu-

tions in contemporary terms;[1] in the novels which relate the pilgrimage of the uprooted townsman in search of his cultural identity. It finds political expression in systems which allow local patriotism a place in the national structure of government. But the local associations of fellow countrymen, like the Ibo unions, articulate the process most clearly in the everyday management of social life. As they confront the problems which beset the homeland or their urban communities, they evolve the principles by which to handle them, at once innovative and conservative in their loyalties.

The process is by its nature ambivalent. It swings between opposing impulses, now reviving the past, now trying to overtake the future, but continually rebounding. It fails when the balance cannot be sustained, and the search for a reconciliation between these impulses is abandoned. The political risks are secession or an uncompromising nationalism, which denies any legitimacy to tribal loyalties whatever. The state may then either be torn apart, or undermined by bitterness and hypocrisy, as tribal influence becomes furtive and corrupt, while the grievances of the excluded are denied expression. The social risks arise from the ambiguity of tribal stereotypes. These stereotypes express, crudely, the diversity of cultures: but in defining the distinctiveness of one's own group, they tend to become moral categories, classing others as inferior. In search of a scapegoat for all manner of frustrations, it is easy to perceive others as not merely inferior, but evil. The effort to accommodate to them then breaks down in rejection or extermination. At one time or another in Ibo history, all these dangers were realised, and Nigeria was nearly destroyed by them.

The viability of tribalism, as a process of mourning for an irretrievable past, is therefore precarious. But it expresses an inevitable conflict, and to condemn tribalism is no more help-

---

[1] In his introduction, Malinowski criticises this: 'At many points unnecessary comparisons are introduced and European expressions such as Church, State, "legal system", "economics", etc., are used with somewhat superfluous implications.' (Kenyatta, 1938, p. xi.) But the comparisons, I believe, make the book more valuable to a modern Kikuyu reader, even if they seem misleading to the professional anthropologist.

ful than exhorting the grief-stricken to pull themselves
together. We need rather to foresee where it will arise, and
find a means of articulating it which will contain the conflicts
and enable them to work themselves out.

THE ORIGINS OF TRIBALISM

Tribalism does not arise simply because people of diverse languages are included within the same formal boundaries. So
long as the state remains loosely integrated, the situations in
which messages must be passed across cultural boundaries can
be isolated, and handled according to conventions which restrict the interaction. These conventions may then develop into
a formal principle of the social order, maintaining a protective
social distance even in a more integrated political and economic system. So, for instance, British settlers in Kenya
resented Africans who presumed to speak to them in English;
and the colonial administration only hesitantly encouraged its
officers to learn the native languages, fearing that this would
impair their detachment. Master and servant, ruler and ruled,
Asian shopkeeper and African customer communicated in a
debased and ungrammatical Swahili, whose range of expression was just enough to exchange routine commands and
requests. The studied impoverishment of the language of inter-
racial relationships reinforced the principle of segregation, re-
stricting what could be said, and isolating it as a special form
of address used only between aliens. By such conventions, social distance can replace distances in space as a means of con-
fining the problems of cultural disparity.

Tribalism, in this sense, appeared in Kenya only as Africans
of different tribes began to settle in towns, where they encoun-
tered each other as equals: it did not become a major factor in
society until the dismantling of the colonial regime.[1] So, too,
tribalism amongst black Americans only became widespread
after the dispersal from the South and civil rights legislation
had narrowed the social and geographical distance between

[1] There had, of course, been intermittent warfare between tribes
in pre-colonial times: but these conflicts were of a different nature
—between societies rather than within them.

themselves and other Americans. Tribalism is a characteristic contemporary phenomenon for these kinds of reasons. Economic development tends to reduce geographical isolation as markets expand, labour moves and becomes more specialised, communications spread and industry is no longer tied to the sources of its fuel. And with this development comes a growing intolerance of the conventions and institutions which uphold social distance. Everywhere but in Southern Africa—which now stands out as the distinctive anomaly in the society of nations—economic integration seems to promote an ideology of cultural equality. So tribalism is likely to emerge most obtrusively in heterogeneous societies whose economies are progressive and whose ideologies are liberal.

At the same time, such societies cannot readily accept it. In the context of national ideals, only the widest possible integration can recruit resources efficiently and arbitrate conflicts over their allocation by common principles of justice. Tribalism seems a residual survival of outdated loyalties—ignorant, parochial and divisive—to be overcome by education and the diffusion of economic opportunity. Yet this is the paradox: though education and development will promote a national consciousness, they thereby reinforce tribal reactions, not disarm them. It was amongst educated Northerners that Colin Legum noticed virulent hatred of the Ibos; and the Ibo Unions were initiated by the most educated and widely travelled amongst the sons of the village. If national institutions cannot acknowledge tribalism as a legitimate expression of social pressures, the resentments can only become subversive, because they cannot be articulated in terms of the governing principles of society. Thus egalitarian, nationalistic ideologies of economic growth generate tensions which they cannot handle, unless they also embody their apparent contradiction.

Suppose, for instance, a civil service is based on impartial recruitment of the ablest staff, irrespective of tribe. If, as is common, education is unevenly distributed, some tribes will be poorly represented. But they cannot legitimately claim a larger share of appointments, unless they can show that tribal prejudice has discriminated against their able candidates. This may be hard to prove, and distorts the issue, frustrating the straightforward expression of a tribal grievance. If, instead, a civil service recognises the principle of tribal balance, then the complaint can be arbitrated. Through such arbitration, case by case, the principles which govern society as a whole become established. Because the conflicts can be articulated within the social structure, there is at least a chance that they can be fought out within the limits of legitimate action. If the leaders of Nigeria, after the first *coup d'état,* had not attempted to abolish the explicitly tribal principles on which the Federation rested, the chain of increasingly desperate reactions which led to war might never have been provoked.

Tribal institutions represent, therefore, a subtle fusion of explicitness and ambiguity. They clarify conflicts by giving them an organisational structure, but express an inherently ambivalent process. They do not resolve contradictory impulses, but contain them within a framework through which a reconciliation can eventually work itself out. To insist that the ambiguity be resolved destroys their function as articulators of a process. Hence they depend on a tolerance of ambiguity in the societies where they arise—a willingness to postpone issues of national commitment and live with ideological inconsistency.

THE VIRTUE OF AMBIGUITY

Let me illustrate the crucial importance of sustaining ambiguity by two examples, where in one the pressures for commitment were resisted, while in the other the issues were disastrously brought to a head. The first is taken from the history of Jewish settlement in England. Here it was the minority who sought clarity of regulation, and the authorities who resisted. But, as James Parkes argues in the essay from which I quote, the failure to define their status enabled the Jewish community to work out, in practice, a position which they would probably have been refused in principle.

In 1655, Manasseh ben Israel, a distinguished Dutch Rabbi, attempted to negotiate the re-establishment of his people in England:

Manasseh came to England and laid before Cromwell himself his plea for the readmission of the Jews. A judicial committee pronounced that there was no law in the statute book

which made it impossible for Jews to reside in the country;
but when it came to the practical discussion of what actually
should be allowed, all the opposition forces raised their
heads and made a formal decision impossible. That Cromwell desired their readmission is certain. . . . But he was
unwilling to force the issue by overriding the opposition. In
consequence, the eloquent plea of Manasseh received no
formal answer, and he returned home to Amsterdam to die,
a disappointed man.

The Jewish community not only received no legal docu-
ment stating the conditions on which they would be formally
permitted to establish themselves and maintain their
religion, but they do not seem to have even received any
written statement from the Protector that they would be permitted to remain in the country, or would be protected
against malicious prosecution in the courts. Nevertheless, he
gave them to understand that the best thing they could do
would be to go on as they were, to remain inconspicuous,
and to trust to his favour. To the Jews of that day it was a
disappointing result of their hopes and endeavours. In fact,
it turned out a blessing. . . . Manasseh and the Jewish leaders themselves, had always assumed that a licensed
resettlement would be on stringent conditions. . . . In fact,
no special taxes, no rights and opportunities, no area of resi-
dence, were ever defined. Disputable issues were allowed to
await decision until they arose out of actual cases.

The fact that there had been no formal law passed under
the Commonwealth which could be repealed at the Restoration emphasised the value of their uncertain status. Charles
II, tolerant by nature, refused to take any steps against them
just as he refused to grant them any formal rights. In
consequence the English Jews of the seventeenth century
had to discover step by step what they could, and what they
could not, do. . . . By such imperceptible means was the re-
establishment of the Jewish community made a fact, without
it ever being subjected to the dangerous possibilities of parliamentary debate. (Parkes, 1955, pp. 10–12.)

Thus English society did not set any formal social distance
between itself and the immigrants, but integrated them into the
economy. Jews were admitted as brokers of the City of London, and could secure public contracts. When it came to the
test, the courts accorded them much the same rights as any

other citizen who practised a nonconformist religion. At the same time, Jewish institutions were powerfully cohesive: like the Ibo Unions, they looked after the social welfare of their poor, built schools and hospitals, imposed fines for breach of community rules. And they were culturally conservative: one hundred and fifty years after their settlement in England, the council of the Sephardi community still kept its minutes in Portuguese, though it had long been a dead language amongst them. This combination of strong tribal institutions, which by splitting and branching continually evolved, with a willingness to leave unresolved ambiguities in the status of Jews, so that irreconcilable issues of principle faded away in a series of pragmatic adjustments, progressively incorporated the Jewish community into English society—despite Fagin and Shylock, and all the popular stereotypes of Jews as grasping, devious and sinister.

My second illustration shows what may happen when ambiguities are challenged. The Asian immigrants to Kenya established their communities under a colonial regime which maintained a formal social distance between races. Their position was secure within a deliberately segregated political and economic structure. It became much more ambiguous with Independence. The Kenya constitution repudiated racial discrimination, promising full citizenship to Asians who applied for it. At the same time, the British Government, doubtful how tolerant an African nation would prove to be, conceded Asians the right to British passports. To work out their future, the Asian communities needed to hold both these alternatives open. They too mistrusted African tolerance. Hostility against them was openly expressed, by educated and uneducated alike, in the conventional stereotypes of racial antagonism: Asians were cunning as hares, were cheats, hypocrites, thieves who would steal from their own brother. Nor, for their part, could they commit themselves wholeheartedly to racial integration. Their prosperity rested upon a commercial network sustained by narrow family and community loyalties, through which credit was guaranteed, business intelligence passed, and relatives provided for. Such a structure could not incorporate African partners without undermining its basis of trust—the sanctions a family could impose upon its members. Thus Asian businessmen could pay only lip-service to Government pressure to Africanise. As I found from a study in Nairobi, they agreed in principle that Asians should help to train and promote Africans in commerce and industry. But in practice, scarcely any employed Africans in positions where they could learn the responsibilities of running a business, and only 4 per cent had taken an African partner, mostly unsuccessfully. If citizenship meant dismantling their commercial network, breaking away from their community institutions and intermarriage, they could never accept it. Yet their businesses were not immediately threatened. The Kenya economy still depended on their skills, and few Africans were ready to replace them (see Marris and Somerset, 1971, pp. 95–6, 252–4).

Thus for the most part, the Asian businessmen we interviewed wanted neither to leave Kenya, nor to commit themselves to Kenya citizenship. They foresaw that Asians would be discriminated against, whether they were citizens or not, and that they would eventually have to surrender their hold over commercial opportunities. But if the process were only gradual enough, they could work out their future. If they had time to ensure their children's education, converting commercial into intellectual capital, the next generation could seek its future anywhere in the world where highly trained skills were in demand. As men retired and their children turned to professions, the communities would gradually disperse, and a remnant would be unobtrusive enough to survive in Kenya. This evolution was possible, so long as the issue of citizenship was not pressed. Nor had any party an interest in pressing it. The Kenya Government was caught between its principles and the virulence of popular prejudice. It did not want to define Kenya as a racially intolerant nation, but it did not want to incorporate an unpopular, culturally alien and economically enviable minority either, and allowed Asian applications for citizenship to lie unanswered. It had to respond to African pressure for greater economic opportunities, in the face of rising unemployment, yet did not want to disrupt the economy by a sudden flight of capital and skills. So, like the Asians themselves, its reactions were ambivalent. Equally, the British Government, given the growing prejudice against coloured immigrants into Britain, found it had made a promise of citizenship which it would be embarrassed either to honour or repudiate.

Such ambiguity is, perhaps, harder to sustain in a discursive democracy than the England of Cromwell or Charles II's day. As discrimination grew in Kenya, and prominent British politicians raised the alarm of mass migration from East Africa, Kenya Asians began to sell up and claim upon their British citizenship while they could. The more they came, the more pressure the British Government faced, until the delicate balance of equivocation collapsed in a panic stricken flight to reach Britain before an act revoking their right of admission was made law. The passage of the Commonwealth Immigration Act was then a foregone conclusion. In effect, Britain, Kenya, the Asians themselves had given pledges of goodwill which, if put to the test, they could not fully honour. So long as these pledges were taken on trust, they sustained the process of transition. Once challenged, the crisis of confidence, like a run on a bank, drove everyone to foreclose their options. Yet it was, I believe, an avoidable tragedy. If the British Government had firmly repeated its promise of an unrestricted right of admission as soon as doubts were raised, there would have been no panic; the Kenya Government need not have demonstrated so insistently that it was not to be deflected from its policy; the rate of migration would have remained manageable; and the issue of the Asian's future would not have been brought to a crisis, where their British rights had to be reinterpreted.[1]

Tribalism, therefore, seeks forms of expression at once explicit and ambiguous, defining—like conventions of mourning—an ambivalent response to change. As political and economic integration promote migration, diffusing opportunities and disrupting traditional patterns of livelihood and government, cultural barriers break down. Tribal institutions are concerned, above all, with the confusion of identity, the loss of

[1] The passage of the Commonwealth Immigration Act probably contributed to the later crisis in Uganda, when Amin expelled most of the Asian population. It obliged the Uganda regime to present an ultimatum intransigent enough to force Britain to relax its restrictions. Without the Act, Asians would have been free to leave spontaneously, the pressure need not have been so extreme, and the evacuation could have been less harassed.

stable meaning in relationships, which arise when people who speak different languages must live together. These differences represent not only the disparity between peoples, but the disparity between a past enclosed within the boundaries of the familiar, and a more open present, potentially rewarding but threateningly unpredictable. When the nations of Europe divided Africa amongst themselves, drawing its tribes together into colonial territories, they provoked these problems of diversity in their most acute form. But the problems also arise where the differences are more subtle: the words are the same, but the patterns of speech and gesture, the categories of thought, the whole style of expression are different. Wherever people are expected to treat each other as equal members of the same society, yet do not share the same symbolic code, the anxieties of misinterpretation create a pervasive defensiveness. I have called these anxieties and the response to them tribalism, since the interaction of tribes in an African nation represents them so clearly. But there are many other situations—from linguistic nationalism to the predicament of black Americans or the intermingling of social classes—where people are similarly threatened.

TRIBALISM AND CULTURAL DISPARITIES BETWEEN UNIVERSITY STUDENTS

To illustrate how an analysis in terms of tribalism can be applied to situations where the cultural disparities are much subtler and less obtrusive than in an African nation, consider the interaction of students at an English university. They arrive there from different kinds of school—fee-paying public schools, grammar schools, comprehensive schools, a few from secondary modern schools—different regions and social backgrounds. Like the newcomers to an African city, they have to decide what offers of friendship they will provisionally accept, what relationships they can safely begin. They look for their own kind, on the basis of signs which are immediately perceptible—accent, manner, dress. Mistaken identification can be embarrassing. To choose the wrong kind of room-mate, or strike up an acquaintanceship which proves abortive is, at best, a tiresome mistake, and at worst involves months of unhappiness to unravel. The greater the differences in style of life the harder is the relationship, because each has to learn a new pattern of expectations and responses to suit the other: jokes fall flat, or give offence; symbols have a different reference; hospitality is exchanged in different kinds of gifts, at different times; the nuances of social behaviour are blunted and confused. These anxieties will be stronger, the more heterogeneous the intake of students, as I found in a comparative study of three English universities early in the nineteen sixties.

At all three universities, some students had noticed social segregation, and described it in terms of stereotyped behaviour: 'There's the clique that must go to the jazz club, whether they want to or not. There's the Bohemian clique, that must dress badly, and so exactly like each other. . . . Also there's a too-too cult here, the new upper-middle class that adopts fashionable attitudes, parties and things like that, and which adopts certain ways of speaking' (Marris, 1964, p. 94). But only a fifth of the students at Southampton, the most homogeneous of the three universities, mentioned such groupings, while at Cambridge, where about half the students had been privately educated and half came from state schools, nearly two-thirds remarked on them. Prejudices were freely expressed, and attached to symbols of dress and manner: check jacket or cavalry twill, college blazer or faded jeans, loud or soft-speaking, 'correct' or aggressively regional accents. Each of these stereotypes had a place or activity with which it was associated—a club, a sport, a pattern of favourite haunts. A student who had enjoyed a sport at school might refuse to play at all at university, just because it belonged to a set with whom he did not wish to identify. Thus the diversity of student society was made manageable by imposing upon it categories of avoidance and affiliation, based on superficial, immediately perceptible signs.

The anxieties which gave rise to these prejudices centred upon language. Students from different social backgrounds felt the strain of communicating across subtle distinctions of class-bounded cultures. They were not conventionally snobbish, but sensed that 'there are very thin but very strong divisions between peoples. You become more aware of the art of being tactful, which imposes a kind of artificiality.' 'I regret that I can't maintain a conversation with these public-school rugby types at John's,' a Cambridge student remarked. 'They don't always understand the way I speak and my accent, and the kind of things we say amongst ourselves. If a person comes from a top public school, and his parents have plenty of money . . . he doesn't speak the same kind of language as chaps like me do.' The awkwardness is reciprocal: 'Friends from the same kind of professional background as myself tend to find it easier to make friends with each other. When I try to make contact with people from a different background, I find it very difficult.' (Ibid., pp. 99 and 100.) Styles of speech were not only barriers to communication, but aspects of personality which students incorporated in their own self-image, and could not readily alter without a sense of betraying their identity. Nearly a third of the Cambridge students said they were self-conscious about their accent, and another quarter had noticed this self-consciousness in others, if not themselves. At worst, this self-consciousness represented a profound anxiety about where they belonged. 'A Cambridge student, for instance, described how "When I'm speaking to the Master, etc., I haven't the courage of my convictions and I tend to iron out my accent. When I came here for interview, I adopted my smoothest accent. I thought that how I said things mattered more than what I said. But on my own level, especially with smoothies and very U-type men, I'm belligerently regional." In reacting against the smoothies, he was also repudiating the smooth-speaking self which he presented to the University authorities. He had created a situation much more damaging to his self-esteem than the mere possession of an uncultured accent, because the contempt was now within himself. Hence he felt—though no one in fact seemed to have given him grounds for thinking so—that "for lots of people at home I'm a sort of social pariah".' (Ibid., p. 96.)

Thus, like migrants to a modern African city, students reacted to each other in terms of the superficial differences of expressive style, which could be perceived at once—accent, clothes, manner of address, what they ate and drank, how they entertained themselves: and they codified these differences in stereotyped categories, which they applied to others but not to themselves. As in Africa, too, the differences arose from the diversity of their cultural backgrounds, according to the school, region and social class of the homes from which they came. The stereotypes helped to define a pattern of avoidance, minimising communication between incompatible styles of self-expression. Not that students from diverse backgrounds never became friends. But the crude categorisation mapped the social field, so that students could steer clear of relationships perceived as awkward and unfamiliar unless they were socially adventurous: the stereotypes provided both signposts and justification, since they were mocking and derogatory. At the same time, the self-consciousness about manner of speech expressed a conflict of loyalties. Students from families without experience of the high culture of an ancient university wanted the intellectual and vocational opportunities it opened for them, without repudiating the values and attachments of their background—as the Ibo Unions had tried to exploit the opportunities of a modern nation and apply their benefits to their homeland. Accent became a means of mediating between these claims—of displaying the intellectual competence of an élite through the expressive style of less pretentiously educated classes. Students who could not sustain this ambiguity often felt they had somehow betrayed themselves. Anyone at their age would be likely to feel the disparity between their sense of self when at home with their parents and when with their contemporaries. But the university both intensified the conflict, by the culture it institutionalised, and added a tribal dimension—especially at Cambridge.

I suggested that tribalism will appear where people of different cultures must treat each other as equals, and cannot get away from each other—where, that is, the social and spatial distance between them is narrow. Although some students at all three universities were preoccupied with accents, and spoke in terms of stereotyped groupings, these reactions were much commoner at Cambridge. The two provincial universities I studied were both comparatively homogeneous. About four-fifths of their students came from grammar schools, and from homes where neither of their parents had received a higher education. But at Cambridge the students were about equally divided between grammar and public school entrants, and nearly half, too, had a university educated mother or fa-

ther. In an academic community, these differences of intellectual background are more sensitive indicators of cultural
style than parents' occupations, since they determine the familiar language a student has grown up with: and in these terms,
Cambridge was much more vulnerable to the anxieties of cultural diversity. At the same time, its collegiate structure drew
students into closer relationships with each other. As members
of a college, they were involved in more intimate communities
than the students at Leeds or Southampton, scattered in lodg-
ings and affiliated only to a single student union. So it was predictable that reactions akin to tribalism should have been more
noticeable at Cambridge. Nor would these reactions have been
provoked in a less liberal community. Many of the students
had experience of National Service, and the diversity of
recruits in an army hut, the intimacy into which they are
herded, are greater than at any university. But the strict hierarchy and regimentation create a highly predictable environment, where individual differences are suppressed.[1]

In none of these English universities did cultural self-
consciousness develop into tribal institutions. Social groups
clustered about favourite activities and meeting places, but the
divisions were not deep enough, nor the anxieties so great as to
overwhelm cross-cutting attachments and create defensive organisations. The conflicts were embodied more in the search
for a personal style—classless, unassuming, but intellectually
aware—which could mediate between home and university. As
a whole, the student community at university represented this
ideal, since even at Cambridge class divisions were regarded as
illegitimate. Outside the university, therefore, students tended
to see themselves collectively as a tribe—alienated by their
sophistication from their less educated family and former

---

[1] The Army also, in a sense, institutionalised tribalism by encouraging loyalty to a regiment, or more narrowly still, to a pla-
toon. But this only superficially resembles tribalism in my sense.
In highly predictable, homogeneous societies, artificial divisions
between groups may be introduced—complete with hostile stereotypes—to provoke team loyalties and competition; and perhaps to
divert hostility from authority. It is a manipulative device, imposed
as a form of social control, and is not spontaneous. Any real inter-
group tension would make it unmanageable.

school mates, but unwilling to identify with a privileged class. At the time of my study, this ambivalence was expressed in their apathy towards conventional politics, and repudiation of any claim to leadership as an élite. Since then, apathy has turned towards a more aggressive assertion of their tribal identity, challenging both the university, as an instrument of acculturation to a privileged class, and the class structure of society as a whole. Thus students and their teachers are increasingly at cross purposes. The students are trying to develop their sense of the university community as an institutional model for society at large, based on their own need to reconcile intellectual achievement with social equality. But their teachers, who are not living through an undergraduate career as a process of reconciliation, see the university only as a means to impart experience and skills for tasks elsewhere.

If the analogy between the prejudices of Cambridge undergraduates and tribalism in Africa seems inconclusive, for lack of any explicit counterpart to tribal institutions, the correspondence is more obvious in America. Here the recruitment of black students to prestigious universities has provoked an insistent demand for such institutions. The situation is essentially similar—a community where people are expected to treat each other as alike, despite manifest differences in expressive style, and where traditional means of maintaining social distance, such as fraternity houses, are in decline. The minority students perceive these differences of style as racial, and race is a powerfully evocative symbol about which to organise. At the Berkeley campus of the University of California, for instance, the black students, with Asian and Mexican support, campaigned successfully for a 'third world' college. Their proposals expressed the ambivalence characteristic of a tribal institution, mediating between the minority and society at large. The college was to have the status of any other college on the campus and share its intellectual reputation, yet it was also to be autonomous, governed exclusively by people of the three ethnic groups, and open without restriction to minority students from the ghettoes. Thus the college, as they conceived it, would have contained the conflicting pressures upon them— at once committed to their own people, asserting their cultural roots and their identification with the struggle to escape from poverty and discrimination; and eager to secure high-ranking academic qualifications. The university authorities found such ambiguity hard to take. They were sympathetic, or at least resigned, to ethnic studies. But they worked within a bureaucratic structure which rested upon liberal but clearly defined rules, and so were continually at odds with the students campaigning for the college. The university wanted to negotiate the unresolved issues, clarifying an agreed structure. To the students, this was a trap, forcing them to abandon one or another of their aims. They angrily refused to recognise the incompatibility between these aims, and in their terms they were justified. The college could not reconcile the conflicting pressures upon them, but it could help to articulate them, and relieve the personal anguish of working the conflict out. Thus the quarrel, which dragged on for months, turned on whether a university could tolerate ambivalent, indeterminate institutions within its structure. It seems that it must, if it is to tolerate ambivalent students: but the implications for the whole administrative hierarchy of a state university are profoundly disturbing.

SUMMARY

In conclusion, it may help to recapitulate the argument briefly. When a student joins a university community, or a villager comes to a modern African city, their self-confidence is threatened by the unfamiliarity of the relationships in which they become involved. They may suffer no more than a brief embarrassment while they still respond awkwardly or get things wrong. But their sense of their own identity may be more profoundly disturbed, if they feel that adaptation requires them to betray their earlier attachments. The university, perhaps, seems to impose an upper middle-class or white suburban culture which denies their nature; the city seems to denigrate the newcomer's background. In such situations, a conflict arises between the yearning to return to the reassuring predictability of the past, and a contradictory impulse to become the creature of circumstance, abandoning the past as if it belonged to another, now repudiated, being. Both impulses are self-destructive in themselves, but their interplay generates the process of reformulation by which the thread of continuity is retrieved. This reformulation of the essential meaning of one's experience of life is a unique reassertion of identity, which takes time to work out. In this it resembles grief: for though the circumstances are not tragic, and the gains may outweigh the losses, the threat of disintegration is similar. Thus slum clearance, colonisation, economic development, divorce, even entering a university may all provoke reactions akin to grief, in so far as they threaten to overwhelm someone's confidence in his or her construction of reality, on which the ability to cope with life depends. (Of course, individuals in such situations will differ in their resilience according to how their past experience has prepared them.)

I do not mean merely that whenever the predictability of the social environment breaks down, people will be bewildered. The process by which they seek to reconstruct a sense of the meaningfulness of life is also fundamentally similar. The ambivalent loyalty to tribal traditions, the students' preoccupation with stereotypes, accents and fear of false commitments, all express the same inherent conflict as bereavement, the same erratic search for a continuity of purpose proof against both self-betrayal and nostalgia—neither to bury the past, nor be buried in it. Tribal associations, like mourning customs, embody these conflicting impulses, defining ways of acting the conflict out which institutionalise a transitional state and insulate it against premature demands that the conflict be finally resolved. They therefore depend on a tolerance of their equivocation by the society which contains them.

Thus the management of change seems to depend on the articulation of conflicting impulses, which must be allowed to work themselves out. The next chapter sets out to define more exactly how mourning customs articulate grief, and how the same principles might be applied to other adjustments to change. At the same time, I try to explain why, in contemporary industrialised societies, we seem to disparage mourning: for I believe this indifference betrays a pervasive insensitivity to all the problems of change we have so far discussed.

V
MOURNING AND THE
PROJECTION OF AMBIVALENCE

If we can understand something about reactions to social changes by thinking of them in terms of bereavement, can we correspondingly learn something about the management of change from mourning customs? At the same time, since contemporary industrial society is extraordinary and perhaps unique in its disparagement of these customs, can we also understand our attitude towards change better by exploring the reasons behind our neglect of them? Never have the bereaved been left to struggle with their grief so little guided by convention. Is it only honesty which leads us to mistrust these ritual gestures, or—as I believe—also muddled unwillingness to recognise loss? Until we have first understood what we are giving up in repudiating any conventional show of grief, and what this rejection expresses, the analogy between mourning and the management of change may still seem strained—a perversely gloomy presentation of the problems of adapting. Let me try to explain why a robust, pragmatic optimism towards change is fundamentally less rational, and indeed tragically blind to the nature of social transitions.

THE DENIAL OF MOURNING

Most societies impose on the bereaved a sequence of ritual acts and conventional behaviour which articulates the process of grieving. As Geoffrey Gorer writes (1965, pp. 112–13):

> The traditional customs of Britain, of all European countries and of very many societies outside the Judeo-Christian tradition prescribe usually in great detail the costume and behaviour appropriate to mourners in the period of intense

mourning after the funeral; they also typically impose an etiquette on all those who come in contact with the mourners; and usually designate the number of days, weeks, months or years that this behaviour should be followed. It is this pattern which I dubbed 'time-limited mourning'; and, on the basis of comparative material from other societies, from the findings of psycho-analysis, and from the material in the foregoing pages, it would appear to be the most appropriate technique for mourners to make the complicated psychological and social adjustments involved in the loss of a primary relative. If these adjustments are not made, the outcome is liable to be the permanent despair of depression or melancholia, an impairment of the capacity to love in the future, or various irrational attitudes towards death and destruction.

The mourning customs of a society express, of course, its particular beliefs about the worlds of the living and the dead, the status of the bereaved, the inheritance of rights and duties. But to the merry or downcast at a funeral, to revenge death or welcome it, to reintegrate widows as the wives of their dead husbands' kinsmen or perpetuate their widowhood are variations on the same ambivalent theme—at once to incorporate the dead and banish them, to retrieve the continuity of meaning in a world of relationships they no longer inhabit. The variety of custom seems to overlay a fundamentally similar structure of support.

First, acts of mourning attenuate the leave-taking. They continue the relationship with the dead, but unlike nostalgic daydreams, or the morbid mummification of the past, do not deny the fact of death. The rituals dramatise death, at once expressing grief and guiding it towards consoling gestures. They enable the bereaved, for a while, to give the dead person as central a place in their lives as they had before: the rituals honour the dead, secure their memory, prepare them for their future in another world—packing baggage, or shriving the soul so that it departs intact upon its journey. To those who believe in an afterlife, these acts may be of the utmost importance, as truly practical a part of the relationship as any that went before. But even when they have become, for most people, conventional rituals without literal purpose, the make-believe of addressing actions to the dead—of laying them to rest, remembering them, caring for them—still helps to express the impulse to hold on to the past, and perhaps to resolve the guilt and anger which death arouses. At the same time, such gestures emphasise death as a crucial event, whose implications must be acknowledged. This transition, from a relationship with a living person to a relationship with a dead person, is the first step in detaching a sense of purpose from its former setting. It makes private grief a public show, which now offends us, but it is much gentler than the blunt assertion that the relationship is over, and one must make the best of it.

Second, mourning customs characteristically mark the stages of reintegration, from withdrawing and assimilating the reality of bereavement, through the painful process of adjustment, to the taking up once more of purposeful relationships. They protect the bereaved from morbid impulses to suppress grief on the one hand, or from taking refuge in a perpetual posture of mourning or nostalgia on the other. In Geoffrey Gorer's phrase, mourning is 'time-limited', both guiding and sanctioning the stages of recovery. Without these conventions, the bereaved are left to struggle unaided with conflicting feelings of guilt—at the unhappiness their state spreads around them, and at the heartlessness and betrayal of the dead that not being unhappy would imply. Several of the widows I interviewed in London described how a remark, by friends at work, a doctor or a priest, urging them to come out of mourning, had relieved their anxiety, as if, denied the reassurance of convention, they clutched at any hint of normative behaviour. At first sight, it seems false to impose custom on so intense and private an emotion as grief; yet the very loneliness of the crisis, and the intensity of ambivalence, cries out for a supportive structure. Both the attenuation of leave-taking and the gradations of customary mourning set a time for the conflicts of grief to work themselves out and sanction their expression, defining the relationship between the bereaved and the rest of society.

But if grief needs to be articulated by custom, why have conventions of mourning behaviour suffered such attrition in contemporary Britain and America? As Gorer concludes from his enquiry (ibid., p. 113):

The most typical reaction of the majority in Britain today (and, as far as my evidence goes, in all English-speaking countries with a Protestant tradition) is the denial of mourning, in the period after the funeral. Certainly, social recognition of mourning has virtually disappeared. . . . Giving way to grief is stigmatised as morbid, unhealthy, demoralising—very much the same terms are used to reprobate mourning as were used to reprobate sex; and the proper action of a friend or well-wisher is felt to be distraction of a mourner from his or her grief; taking them 'out of themselves' by diversions, encouraging them to seek new scenes and experiences, preventing them 'living in the past'. Mourning is treated as if it were a weakness, a self-indulgence, a reprehensible bad habit instead of a psychological necessity.

Not that the customs have altogether gone: over half the bereaved he interviewed, for instance, wore some token of mourning, and two-fifths of those who had lost a husband or wife wore mourning for at least three months. In my own study, most of the widows—and especially the older women—wore mourning for three months or more. But many of the younger women expressed the same disrespect for mourning customs which Geoffrey Gorer noticed. 'Personally, I don't believe in all that,' as one told me. 'Once you're dead, you're dead. There's nothing else. I remember my husband once said, "Don't make a fuss when I'm gone." ' Others, too, quoted their husband's authority for their opinion: 'For God's sake, if anything happens to me, don't go about like that' (in black); 'Don't keep coming putting flowers on my grave, I won't be able to smell them.' (Marris, 1958, p. 35.) This bleak rationality derives in part from disbelief in an afterlife—a conventional religious agnosticism which robs acts of mourning of their literal meaning. It reflects too, perhaps, the privacy of family life in modern urban society, where the display of private distress seems out of place—a loss of self-control. But it also seems to represent a more general attitude towards loss which, from the standpoint of this essay, is not as rational as it first appears.

Urging the bereaved to 'make the best of it' only makes sense so long as 'best' still has meaning for them. It presup-

poses some essential purpose, invulnerable to loss, by which
better or worse actions can still be discriminated. For younger
widows, this purpose is typically taken to be the care of their
children: but more generally, I think it is conceived in the
vaguest and most abstract terms—to be happy, to be active and
interested. Neither of these purposes can at first reassure a
widow. She recognises her duty towards her children, but while
she is overwhelmed by grief there is little psychic reward in
fulfilling it: her role as mother is so integrated with her role as
wife that she cannot simply extricate the meaning of one from
the other. And to be happy is so undirected an aim, it becomes
impersonal. Officious comforters speak of taking the bereaved
'out of themselves'—as if in recognition that consolation
implies anonymity, a capacity for enjoyment alienated from
any sense of the meaning of a particular life. People can
indeed find occasional relief in self-forgetting, but the consolation is insidiously empty. The distaste for mourning is, I think,
influenced by a secular hedonism, which seeks to banish the
possibility of loss from normal life by a form of emotional
sophistry.

I have argued that as grief works itself out, a sense of purpose is gradually detached from the relationship which incorporated it, and so reformulated that it can once again interpret
events. This reconstruction of meaning is painful, because it
begins in such helplessness and uncertainty. But conversely, if
purposes can be conceived in sufficiently abstract terms, they
will never become dependent on a particular context: the abstraction supposes an indeterminate variety of circumstances,
each substitutable for another, to which these purposes are relevant. There is, I think, a universal temptation to seek this ultimate invulnerability; to define the meaning of life in such detachment from mortality that nothing can ever touch the core
of being. But the search is self-defeating, because every choice
commits purposes to particular relationships, and only in that
context do we learn what we mean by those purposes. Without
choosing, nothing ever means very much: the uncommitted
person is deadened by a perpetual fear of bereavement, and
learns only the futility of this evasion.

Secular societies in the Protestant tradition tend, I think, to
let their collective sense of purpose degenerate into such bland

vacuity, because commitment is conceived to be a matter of personal choice, which should not be pre-empted by any public direction. (Conversely, reforms with a clear sense of what these collective purposes should be tend to repudiate the tradition. Roland Warren explores these contrasting points of view in his essay *Truth, Love and Social Change*.) Hence the common image becomes an unspecific hedonism: the advertisers' world of aimlessly happy people doing nothing in particular in neutral surroundings. Correspondingly, we share a common image of deprivation and unhappiness as the absence of this indeterminate well-being, but no conception of loss. Grief seems the futile indulgence of misery: we accept the need for it without understanding, unable to acknowledge the intense psychic effort involved in the reconstruction of real purpose, impatient with its rejection of consolation. We make mourning seem meaningless by appealing to an aimless collective hedonism which in itself can give no meaning to any experience.

Thus the denial of mourning can be interpreted as a perverse outgrowth of the Protestant tradition, unwittingly contradicting its original insight. Protestantism stems from the insistence that religious truth can only be grasped through personal experience: the meaning of God's design becomes apparent in the day to day business of life, as men and women seek to affirm their salvation. This doctrine recognises, at least by implication, that purposes inhere in specific attachments, and have no real meaning apart from them. But at the same time, it also implies a tolerance of individual constructions of meanings which progressively empties collective statements of purpose of any particularity. It draws the boundaries of permitted behaviour in terms of the most general principles of rationality and humanity. This utilitarianism comes to be mistaken for the very attitude towards personal experience that Protestantism originally repudiated. Abstracting notions of goodness from specific patterns of behaviour creates the illusion that relationships can be substituted one for another, and so ignores the nature of loss. We confuse the collective conception of a good life—which is increasingly indeterminate and open-minded— with individual conceptions, which are bound to particular attachments. Whenever, as in advertising, we put forward public images of private enjoyment, the images are inevitably insipid and divorced from any real context. So we promote the fallacy that happiness lies in conforming to these notional symbols of satisfaction.

If this utilitarian outlook inhibits our understanding of bereavement, it blunts our sensitivity to the implications of social changes even more. Public exhortations to growth, progress, revolution seldom specify what they mean, since any specification would affront the essential privacy of moral choice, the supremacy of individual interpretations of commitment. This abstraction of principle permits a tolerant, pluralistic conception of society. But it tends, I think, to confuse the diversity of meaningful relationships which society can comprehend with the diversity which an individual life can comprehend. It mistakes the principles which sustain the openness of society for those which sustain the lives of its members. It does not follow, because the aims of a pluralistic society as a whole can only be described in very general, unspecific terms, that the same must be true for its constituents. The essence of the Protestant tradition is that people should be free to make their own commitments—to elaborate a structure of meaning to their lives which will be a truer expression of their humanity and a truer basis of unity, because it is generated out of their own experience.[1] The tolerance and adaptability of society as a whole depends upon the security of these commitments. For if people cannot protect their personal sense of identity, they will begin to demand that the social framework itself should provide the structure of meaning they cannot find in their own experience. Thus the recognition of grieving, as a natural response to loss, matters most to those societies which most respect liberty of conscience. But it is in these societies, too, that the logic of religious toleration has made for a curious blindness to the reality of bereavement. Just as we discount the symbols of

[1] As Oliver Cromwell wrote of his New Model Army: 'All that believe have the real unity, which is most glorious because inward and spiritual. . . . As for being united in forms, commonly called uniformity, every Christian will for peace sake study and do as far as conscience will permit, and from brethren, in things of the mind, we look for no compulsion but that of light and reason.' Quoted in Hill (1970, p. 74).

mourning, because they no longer have a universal meaning, so we discount loss, because it is merely private and particular. The residual utilitarianism of our common principles suggests a substitutability of satisfactions, whose spurious rationality cannot comprehend grief.

This belief that loss can be made good by substitution is, I think, reinforced by the predominantly bureaucratic organisation of contemporary industrial society. The crucial administrative structures no longer depend upon familial structures, but on the co-ordination of impersonal functions. Bureaucracies are impregnable by death. At worst it robs them of experienced talent which may be scarce. The organisation itself is hardly disturbed—the dead man's replacement is already waiting. A bureaucratic society, therefore, need not prescribe the passage of mourning: death creates no crisis in its corporate life. So we come to perceive grief as a sickness because, in terms of the dominant principles of our social organisation, the unwillingness to replace a vacated role promptly is as much an aberration as the unwillingness to substitute for a missing satisfaction.

Freud caught the spirit of this baffled rationalism when he remarked that the pain of grief was 'not at all easy to explain in terms of mental economics'. There seems, indeed, no profit in it. Where we once conceived the search for meaning as the intense, private struggle to interpret God's design, we see it now in terms of alternative markets for our psychic investment, indifferent to anything but the rate of return—even literally, when we reduce the costs and benefits of change to money.

If we believe that the meaning of life can only be defined in the particular experience of each individual, we cannot at the same time treat that experience as indifferent—uprooting people from their homes, disrupting their relationships with impatiently facile exhortations to adaptability. Such change implies loss, and these losses must be grieved for, unless life is meaningless anyway. Thus the management of change depends upon our ability to articulate the process of grieving. I have tried to understand why we seem to have trivialised this problem. But if we do not know how to mourn, we cannot know how to live; and the diffuse distress of unacknowledged grief will destroy our liberalism and our respect for life.

Without this sensitivity to the implications of loss, any conception of change becomes callously destructive. But mourning customs relate only to death, and their symbols represent a particular interpretation of now and hereafter, as well as an intuition of the universal nature of grief. How can they be reinterpreted as principles for the assimilation of change?

THE ARTICULATION OF AMBIVALENCE

Once we recognise that loss cannot be made good merely by substitution, the logic of mourning becomes apparent. If life is to seem meaningful again, it is not enough that the present should still be notionally worthwhile. The bereaved must be able to identify, in each concrete event they experience, some response worth making. The vitality of that response depends upon a commitment of purpose, which has already been given and cannot now be wished away, even though the relationships which incorporated it have been disrupted. Hence, as I have tried to show, grief works itself out through a process of reformulation, rather than substitution. Confidence in the original commitment is restored by extracting its essential meaning and grafting it upon the present. This process involves repeated reassurances of the strength and inviolability of the original commitment, as much as a search for the terms on which reattachment would still make life worth living. Until this ambivalent testing of past and future has retrieved the thread of continuity, it is itself the only deeply meaningful activity in which the bereaved can be engaged. Conventions of mourning acknowledge this, giving form and status to grief, protecting the bereaved from demands for responsive behaviour which they are not yet ready to make.

Mourning for a death is a special instance of the management of loss, but its principles can be generalised. It recognises, first, that loss generates a conflict which must be worked out, so as to restore a vital sense of continuity to experience; second, that the resolution of this conflict cannot be preordained, since the resolution only becomes meaningful through the ambivalent exploration by which it is realised; and so, finally, that until grief is worked out, the conflict itself becomes the only meaningful reference for behaviour. Thus changes in society create a need for institutions able to embody these same principles.

I argued earlier that one of the distinctive virtues of tribalism is its ability to institutionalise ambiguity. Tribal associations grapple with all the unresolved issues of change—how people of different languages are to relate to each other, how their traditions are to merge in a nation, how family loyalties are to be reconciled with loyalty to the state. Their responses are characteristically equivocal; and this ability to contain contradictory impulses institutionalises the search for an ideology that will ultimately reconcile past and future. At the same time, they protect their members from the complexity of these issues by prescribing, in terms of tribal loyalty, a predictable set of behaviour—as mourning customs, by analogy, prescribe behaviour appropriate to the unresolved conflicts of grief. The tribesman who associates with his compatriots in the heterogeneous city, pays his dues and follows the rules of membership, can interpret the everyday demands of life, without confronting within his own nature the underlying incompatibilities in the meaning of social relationships.

Thus tribal associations create boundaries which help to define relationships. The boundaries do not resolve the problems of social coherence. But they protect people from having to confront the confusion as an aspect of their own uncertain identity, unmediated by any given sense of where they belong. If these boundaries are threatened, the tensions will once again press upon people directly, and may provoke panic-stricken violence or flight. Conversely, the more nakedly people are exposed to the anxieties of change, the more uncompromisingly they will try to erect protective barriers about their precarious sense of self. That is, they may seek to invent a 'tribe'—a collective identification—where none has existed, and project their internal conflict upon society in these terms.

This process of externalising ambivalence is, I think, a crucial aspect of the management of change. Let me give two further illustrations, which differ from the Ibo associations in that the basis of a collective identification was not already present in a social tradition. The boundaries had first to be drawn. The first illustration shows how the process can work itself out in ideological terms, when internal conflict is

projected as the central fact of the external world, and so re-
stores a meaningful frame of reference for behaviour.

IDEOLOGIES OF CONFLICT

One of the most powerful expressions of the search for boundaries is Franz Fanon's famous essay on decolonisation, *Les
Damnés de la terre*. As a revolutionary statement, its theme is
the loss of identity which colonisation inflicted on the
colonised, and the redemption of that identity through violent
struggle. Yet its intellectual style is strikingly at odds with its
central message—the need to repudiate absolutely and
violently the European culture with which the essay is itself
imbued. This ambiguity represents, I suggest, a much more
personal loss—the disillusionment of a black intellectual, who
had seen his ideals betrayed. The argument of the essay can be
seen both as a projection of grief, and an attempt to escape its
painful ambivalence by a rationalisation of conflict. Fanon
idealises violence, because he can find no other way of expur-
gating the tensions inherent in his own identity.

Fanon was a black Martiniquan, a doctor and intellectual of
the French left, who became an agent of the Algerian liberation movement. In each aspect of his career, his faith had been
abused. He had seen French doctors deny the practice of torture they had witnessed with their own eyes; black poets who
had celebrated the distinctive quality of negritude welcoming
half-hearted independence within the French community. He
had watched the French Communist Party align itself against
the Algerian rebels; and the emergence of an exploitative bour-
geois élite within the newly independent African states. Everyone else, as the crisis of decolonisation progressed, had found
where they belonged, protecting themselves against the contradictory pressures of reintegration. But Fanon, the displaced intellectual and political outsider, had no tribal refuge. He still
had to face the conflict as a personal crisis of identity.

It is this loneliness, this naked exposure to the ambiguities of
decolonisation, which leads him to identify with those he per-
ceives as equally betrayed, the oppressed mass of the people.
Until the intellectual makes common cause with the peasant
folk he cannot find himself again. But these 'wretched of the

earth' appear in his essay only as an undifferentiated and idealised symbol of innocence—a latent, uncorrupted meaning of life that must reassert itself through the annihilation of the colonial experience. Hence the appeal to violence. 'It is struggle which, by exploding the old colonial reality, reveals its hidden aspects, gives rise to new meanings and puts its finger on the contradictions camouflaged by that reality. . . . Only violence exercised by the people, violence organised and enlightened by leadership allows the masses to decipher the reality of society, and gives them the key to it.' (Fanon, 1968, p. 94.) Violence is thus to Fanon an assertion of meaning, rather than an act of destruction. It represents both the impulses of grief, for it is at once an annihilation of the past—a new beginning—and a reassertion of the original humanity which colonisation overwhelmed. At the same time, violence is a symbol of the commitment that will banish the ambiguities and make a person whole. 'At the individual level,' he claims, 'violence purges the colonised of his inferiority complex, of his passive or desperate attitudes; it makes him brave, rehabilitating him in his own eyes.' (Ibid., pp. 51–2.) But this insight into the psychological destructiveness of colonisation idealises violence, which cannot itself ensure the reintegration he claims for it.

In practice, as Fanon knew, violence only plunges a confused identity into deeper conflict. Elsewhere in the book, he describes from clinical observation how those who torture and commit acts of terrorism have been haunted thereafter by these acts. 'His psychiatric case histories concern not only the victims, but also the perpetrators of violence. An African militant had planted a bomb in a cafe, killing ten. Every year, at about the same time, he suffered from acute anxiety, insomnia and suicidal obsessions. An Algerian whose own mother had been wantonly murdered himself wantonly killed a white woman who was on her knees begging for mercy. As a result, he suffered what Fanon calls an anxiety psychosis of the depersonalisation type.' David Caute, from whom I have quoted, comments, 'Fanon's own close involvement and understanding of such cases makes his theory of renovating violence more difficult to understand.' (Caute, 1970, pp. 87–8.)

But the violence is at heart directed against himself. The harshness of the rhetoric betrays the intensity of the ambivalence it seeks to resolve. The myth of violence dramatises the contradictions and helps to contain them within an ideology of struggle. But it remains a projection, displacing not resolving the internal ambivalence. Though Fanon repudiates Europe with contempt, he still writes for the civilisation he rejects. He speaks to the guilt and moral uncertainty of European liberalism, to the hopes and frustrations of those entangled in its equivocal promises. However bravely Fanon salutes the masses of Africa as his comrades in arms, he cannot help being also on the other side: for in his struggle to make sense of life, his only resources are an intellectual command of a wholly European tradition of thought. The revolutionary ideals against which he judges the leadership of independent African states are still those of the French left. He turned to Jean-Paul Sartre, whose conversation he loved, not to a leader of the Algerian resistance, for a preface to his book. Its power lies, I think, in the passionate sincerity with which it expresses these contradictions, and contains them within a web of argument.

The rationalisation of conflict, like mourning customs and tribal institutions, mediates between the disorientation of bereavement and the resolution of grief. I am supposing—as the circumstances of his life and the tone of his writing suggest—that Fanon confronted a crisis where his cultural and professional attachments could no longer be reconciled with his identification with the victims of colonisation. When such contradictions are experienced so acutely as to overwhelm any incremental adjustment, the sense of loss can be as traumatic as bereavement by death or dispossession. Grief then overlays these conflicts with another—between the effort to recapture the meaningful world before the loss, and to abandon the past altogether. While this conflict is working out, it is itself the only deeply meaningful reference for behaviour. Mourning customs institutionalise this meaning, for in performing them, the bereaved both express their continuing attachment to the dead, and take leave of them. The structure of Fanon's thought provides a corresponding external reference for internal conflict. The argument is a violent leave-taking from any attachment to European culture, yet his own intellectual attachment to it is still profound, and the essay everywhere displays it. But as intepreter of the conflict he can find an intermediate meaning, which contains without resolving the impulses of grief. In time, had he lived, he would I think have moved towards a reformulation which did not deny so absolutely the possibility of incorporating his intellectual inheritance in a non-European identity.

This is not to deny the validity of his insight into the psychological consequences of colonisation. But as a way of grasping the reality of one's situation, it is meaningful especially to those who share a similar cultured bereavement. Fanon influenced leaders of the black power movement in the United States. (See for instance Carmichael and Hamilton, 1969, pp. 14–15.) That movement, too, draws an uncompromising boundary, bitterly rejecting the American civilisation of which it is still a part, and with which it is still trying to come to terms. The symbolic identification with Africa only puzzles Africans: but white Americans can understand it, because it arises from a tradition of cultural pluralism which they share. Black rage and white guilt together project an image of conflict which expresses a mutual sense of betrayal. This ideology of conflict is not simply a response to the reality of deprivation and discrimination: it does not press claims or demand rights only for their own sake, but to sustain the conflict itself. Its intransigence wards off the unbearable strain of incorporating the contradictions, and cannot help being identified with both sides. The poor know who they are: they have lost nothing because they have gained nothing. For them conflict is a less ambiguous struggle for the goods of life. But for their champions, the poor and oppressed are symbols of dispossession, with which their own sense of loss becomes identified. They are inconsolable for a deprivation they may never have experienced. Then, like the bereaved in the crisis of grief, even the possibility of consolation seems a betrayal.

Is this perhaps why the ideal of revolution as an irreconcilable opposition of classes has such a powerful appeal for those who have lost their sense of belonging? And why, within this intellectual tradition, the emphasis tends to be on the rejection of compromise, the inevitability of conflict, rather than the form of the ultimate reconciliation to which conflict will lead? This ideological emphasis is, I think, characteristically an

expression of mourning: it denies any meaning to the present
except in terms of the disintegration of any worthwhile purpose, and projects the struggle to recover purpose on society as
a whole, less concerned with the outcome than with articulating the conflict itself. To those who do not share the sense of
loss, the vision seems paranoid. But to those who do, it relieves
the threat of personal disintegration, because the structure of
conflict offers a side to take, a reference for behaviour, a meaning to the experience of loss: and with this reassurance, life
becomes manageable again, and the ambivalence less oppressive. At its most extreme, this perception of reality leads to a
symbolic identification with schizophrenia. For once the internal contradictions are projected and the mad are seen as the
victims of contradictions in society, they become the martyrs
of a universal condition, their heroic struggle the only truly
meaningful existence. These ideologies of conflict are, I think,
fundamentally different from revolutionary ideologies which
attempt to formulate a resolution of the conflict. For the latter
violence and struggle are questions of strategy; for the former
they are the heart of the matter.

Thus ideologies of conflict, like tribal institutions or mourning customs, externalise the ambivalence of loss. They create a
framework in which actions can have meaning although the
ambivalence is still unresolved. I do not mean to imply that the
conflict is therefore an unreal imposition. To see the world in
terms of irreconcilable conflict is neither true nor false, only
necessary or unnecessary to the sense one can make of it. But I
think ideologies of conflict, by protecting the inner sense of
identity against disintegration, can in time lead people to con-
template the possibility of reconciliation again.

CONFLICTS AS THE WORKING OUT OF GRIEF

This need to project ambivalence will influence the response to
reforms, even when the changes are less dramatic and pervasive than decolonisation. For if any reform is to change relationships, it is likely to provoke tensions which can be relieved
by drawing the boundaries of a conflict. Conflict is a very powerful organising principle of behaviour, simplifying and clarifying immediate purposes. As people take sides, they can in-

terpret their response to the situation in terms of this opposition. Yet the partisan commitment is only possible, because the opponents uphold purposes which both sides at heart acknowledge to be valid. Thus each party is looking for some reconciliation of contradictory impulses, but each protects its partisans from the threat to their personal integrity, by translating the internal conflict into a contest beween two more or less coherent groups. I am not suggesting that all social conflicts are projections of an ambivalent reaction to loss: they may represent a straightforward competition of interests. Rather, the institutionalising of conflicting interest groups is the outcome of the process I am describing, which begins as an anxious search for boundaries. So when reforms create confusion in relationships, they are likely to be more manageable when they allow a structure of oppositions to evolve.

This is a hard truth for reformers to accept, I think. To them, their proposals are already the resolution of a problem, which represents the public interest. The success of the changes seems to depend on goodwill and mutual understanding; conflict only frustrates the co-operation that will best serve everyone. But this attitude betrays the rationalism which makes any form of grieving unintelligible. If changes are disruptive, they do not become at once assimilable just because they may be good sense. The continuity of understanding has still to be restored, by testing what relationships now mean in terms which can be derived from what they used to mean.

From this point of view, let me describe briefly some of the strains inherent in American community action programmes, as they influenced the participation of representatives of the poor. Compared with the sweep of Franz Fanon's ideology, this second illustration is small in scale: but here, too, confrontation served a need similar to the idealisation of violence. Though the scope of the community action programmes was modest enough, they implied a radical change in the relationship between elected authority and its constituency—a new conception of democratic interaction, beyond the right to vote and lobby. Representatives of the poor were recruited to the boards of these community agencies, so that they could formulate the needs of their people and work out an agreed plan of action with politicians, planners and professional administrators. Such a proposal was bound to upset everyone's preconceptions.

When people formerly without influence were invited to participate in decisions, they lost their irresponsibility. All their familiar attitudes to authority were invalidated. They were now the colleagues of administrators, not merely the clients of their services. They could no longer regard established power as beyond their control, a given factor of their circumstances. They sacrificed the old freedom of apathy or dissent for an influence whose rewards were unpredictable. Yet if they were to act as authentic representatives of their people, they had still to be able to interpret life as those without power experienced it. Hence they were caught between the familiar, irresponsible relationship to authority they had lost, and a role as responsible reformer, where they risked betraying both themselves and their constituency. Only a personality of exceptional integrity could contain such tension; only a politician of exceptional insight could have foreseen how to formulate a meaningful strategy in so untried a setting.

Established authorities, too, had to modify their familiar conceptions of control and were caught in a corresponding ambivalence. They were continually tempted to revert to more habitual dealing—by-passing discussion, pre-empting decisions —yet some at least were sincerely committed to the ideal of participatory democracy. To reformulate relationships of government within the city, old conceptions could not simply be abandoned. The ideals and loyalties they represented would have to be reincorporated. The legitimacy of elected government, the struggle against racial discrimination, the alienation of the poor—each familiar aspect of political reality had to be revised within the framework of participation.

Like the insensitive well-wishers who urge the bereaved to pull themselves together and make the best of it, the design of community action ignored this ambivalence. It assumed that once people had agreed to take part, they would engage unequivocally in the tasks of planning, not as adversaries but colleagues, arguing rationally over their differences. Hence it placed the community representatives in a situation where they had to internalise all the ambiguities of their position. Some passively endorsed the plans put forward, overwhelmed by the burden of assimilating them to their own perceptions; others reacted against the threat of co-option by angry outbursts against the whole approach. To the promoters of community participation, the experience was disillusioning. The representatives of the poor often seemed destructive and disunited; the representatives of government devious and insincere. The community action agency found itself the principal target of attack from the very people it was trying to help. Because the initial structure of participation did not recognise divisions, no one could relate to it while their own impulses were so confused.

For the most part, the struggles to define the issues ended in mutual frustration and exhaustion. But in a few cities, where community groups were able to define themselves in opposition to city hall, a process of bargaining began to emerge, from which some meaningful reform of power relationships could evolve. As the boundaries were consolidated, participation no longer threatened people so intimately, and they could negotiate in the spirit of adversaries. At first sight, the retreat from mutual discussion into confrontation seems to defeat the ideal of democratic participation. But it would be impossible, I think, ever to make important changes in relationships of government without such a process of withdrawing, so to speak, behind the protection of tribal barriers. Once the lines of conflict were drawn, forms of accommodation could be tested.

If conflict can represent the ambivalence of loss, so the working out of conflict can represent a process similar to grieving. The interaction leads both sides to reinterpret their essential purposes, by successive approximation, in the form of negotiable propositions. As each side states its case, it is at once reasserting the inviolability of its principles, and seeking to impose its own construction of reality on its opponents. Even at the outset, the statement of a case involves some concession to the opposing point of view, since it can only offer a convincing argument in terms the opposition understands (or, at least, an argument that some third party, with influence over the opposition, will understand). Each side borrows from the language and principles of the other to drive its point home, subtly modifying its own stand: every refutation is also a revision. At the same time, the conflict generates rules of behaviour which define its limits. Each side acts as if the other is susceptible to accusations of unfair tactics, defending itself against such accusations in return, and so they converge upon a common conception of legitimacy. The issues are narrowed until they become contained within a frame of reference which defines the nature of the sanctions either side may use, the shared assumptions, what arguments must be accepted or facts acknowledged, the procedures of arbitration. None of these may be known or agreed at the outset. But as such principles are established, they restore the predictability of relationships and make sense of them. Thus the routinisation of conflict can itself resolve the ambivalence of loss.

The same analysis can be applied to the strategy of coalition. Community groups, once they had defined their conflict with city hall, found that their interests could not be presented merely as neighbourhood issues, within the scope of local community action. If they were to achieve any important influence, they needed to bring pressure to bear on national policies. Disadvantaged minorities would have to concert their strategy. But this raised again all the anxieties of ambiguous boundaries. Suppose, for instance, that the Spanish-speaking minorities—Mexican, Puerto Rican, Cuban exiles—try to make common cause. They hold a national conference at which each group puts forward its resolutions. Many of these resolutions express symbolic issues, which are important to the collective identity of one group, but not the others. Each then feels threatened if its symbolic issues are not endorsed, but is at the same time wary of committing itself to issues which do not mean much to its own members. If the conference tries to act as one, passing resolutions by majority vote, it may break up in anger and confusion because the boundaries which define the separate identity of each group have not been respected. A majority can reject a proposal; but if it refuses to recognise the validity of the experience from which that proposal derives, it becomes destructive. To negotiate a common platform, the constituent parts must first be confident that no resolution will overwhelm their right to be themselves. If the groups are intrinsically insecure, still unsure of their integrity and purpose, any alliance may seem threatening.

Thus community action has to evolve through a politics of identity formation into a politics of interests. It is, characteristically, an erratic process, where negotiation is always liable to threaten the internal coherence of one side or the other, provoking a reaction towards the reasserting of differences. As an attempt to reconstruct relationships of government, it fails when it refuses to recognise boundaries, frustrating the externalising of ambiguity: and it fails if, when the lines are drawn, it cannot generate enough confidence in these collective identities to move people from defensive self-assertion to negotiation. As in bereavement, the process of assimilating loss is abortive when conflict is denied or when it becomes stuck in a posture of inconsolability.

Slum clearance, as I suggested earlier, is a bad strategy of social change just because it makes loss so difficult to articulate in any coherent social conflict. In Lagos, for instance, the residents fought vigorously against eviction. But once their resistance failed, and they had lost their homes, they were scattered and demoralised. They grieved in isolation; and the evidence of their bereavement only served as propaganda for those who had not yet been cleared, reinforcing the intransigence of the opposition. Thus the continuing struggle against the scheme did not help its victims, but reminded them vividly of their loss. An opportunity was provided, however, by the provisions of the scheme, for former owners to repurchase land in the cleared area after it had been redeveloped. Although the proposed charges and building standards made it virtually impossible for any owners to claim their option, here at least was an issue that could be joined. Those who undertook the fight for better terms were, I think, much less demoralised by eviction, even though the concessions they exacted never adequately met their case.

In the same way, ideologies of conflict enable those overwhelmed by the confusion of change to take their bearings, but lead towards ideologies which express a strategy for reconstruction. The ambivalence of loss is transformed into a conflict of interests. As these conflicts become institutions, governed by predictable conventions of behaviour, they come themselves to express the meaning of relationships. They are likely thereafter to maintain themselves with all the tenacity of the conservative impulse. The conservatism of organisations derives largely from the routinisation of hostility, by which each position in the hierarchy defends the familiar structure of relationships—and those who play the game most aggressively, least troubled by concern for the organisation as a whole, seem most at ease. Hence the conflicts which represent the working out of grief need not find their resolution in whole-hearted social reintegration: they may as well restore a sense of continuity and meaningful purpose by the articulation of controversy.

I have tried to show how the internal conflict of grief becomes more manageable, when it is projected as a social drama to which people can relate their behaviour. It seems to me that we often do the opposite, trying to suppress the expression of ambivalence from fear of social conflict. If people can be made to swallow their grief, changes will seem superficially less disruptive. But then we cannot comprehend the conservatism which seems, at every turn, to resist the facile rationality of our strategy of reform; nor the violence which bursts out of all the internal contradictions. When loss cannot be articulated, its suppressed tensions will in the end prove more profoundly disruptive than the social conflicts which relieve them.

Above all, if we deny grief, we deny the importance of the meaning each of us has struggled to make of life. Loss is painful because we are committed to the significance of our personal experience. However it is disrupted, we cannot then escape the inner conflicts of bereavement, unless we cultivate a deadening indifference: we cannot refuse to recognise this bereavement in others, without contempt for their sense of life. Perhaps this is obvious, but I think it is often overlooked.

This insistence that grief is an inevitable response to losses which cannot readily be assimilated raises a critical question. People sometimes freely initiate changes which severely disrupt the familiar context of their lives, and expose themselves to the conflicts of bereavement. Why do they jeopardise their peace of mind? Unless this can be explained within the terms of my argument, I have over-stated the case.

VI

THE CONSERVATISM IN INNOVATION

If the conservative impulse is so pervasive, why should anyone willingly risk the uncertainties of innovation? The situations presented in the preceding chapters imply that innovation occurs in response to crucial loss. To reconstruct our understanding of life, reforming the relationships and institutions to embody it, is too disturbing a task to undertake unless circumstances force us to confront it. Our instinct of survival pulls us the other way, to protect our sense of identity and the setting which has moulded it. New institutions, such as the Ibo tribal associations, are provoked by bereavement—innovative by default, as they struggle to retrieve a thread of continuity. But all innovation cannot obviously be explained as a reaction to disruptive alien intrusions. Reforms, rebellions, new styles in art, new theories in science, exploration and technical invention are as commonplace as the resistance to them: the conservatism of institutions would hardly show, unless they were continually challenged. Can this restless impatience with familiar ways be reconciled with the conservative impulse?

The need to conserve the structure of purposes which makes life meaningful does not in itself preclude the development of new skills or the exploration of new experiences. Rather, as I suggested in the first chapter, growth rests on the durability of the expectations we have already learned to trust. The more secure we feel, the more open to experience, so long as we believe it will enlarge rather than undermine our understanding. We can readily accommodate to changes, so long as they can first be assimilated to our existing patterns of thought and attachment. But the changes we initiate are not always conceived as extending and elaborating the already established principles of our lives. Some seem deliberately to repudiate habitual assumptions, overturning expectations and questioning relationships, in ways which are disruptive to ourselves as well as others. Why, if we so often vehemently resist such changes, and succumb to them with grief, should we also sometimes initiate them without apparent pressure of circumstances?

Since the line of thought I want to follow was first suggested by a study of African businessmen in Kenya, which Anthony Somerset and I made a few years ago, I will begin by describing briefly this instance of entrepreneurial innovation. Even if such small African enterprises are not yet in themselves very influential, economic entrepreneurship is, in general, one of the most obvious agents of disruptive social changes; and it is characteristically autonomous—a spontaneous initiative never wholly determined by economic circumstance, nor predictable as the expected development of talent or resources. Entrepreneurs provide, then, an example of change apparently not accountable in terms of a conservative impulse, nor related to any loss, yet too unsettling, too fraught with risks, to be treated simply as the extension of a confident personality. I want to show, however, that the African entrepreneurs we studied were in a sense reacting to loss after all, and had to struggle with problems of identity analogous to the process of grieving. If so, the question remains whether the same might be said of entrepreneurship elsewhere; and indeed of other kinds of innovation. Is innovation itself, paradoxically, an attempt to restore the continuity of expectations?

THE ORIGINS OF AFRICAN ENTREPRENEURSHIP

Over the past forty or fifty years, many thousand small African businesses have grown up in the market centres of the Kenya countryside, often failing and changing hands. Much more recently, distinguished Africans have been appointed to the boards of European companies, while young graduates of high school and university have been recruited to their management staff. But the innovative businessmen are rather those who, since Independence, have pioneered wholesaling, small-scale manufacturing and service industries which Africans never before had the chance to own. At the time of our study in 1967 there were fewer than two hundred of them. The enterprises were not, in themselves, new to Kenya: Indians and Europeans had run garages, sawmills, bakeries, dry cleaning shops since the 1930s. But the African newcomers had to find different markets and forms of organisation, for which there was no familiar guide. In this sense they were innovators, and they saw themselves as promoting an original contribution to Kenya's development. They struggled with problems of management, finance, and access to markets which could not be solved in European or Asian terms, because African ownership created a different pattern of relationship. The risks were therefore largely unpredictable, and the workable principles of African business organisation had to be discovered by experiment.

The men who accepted these risks were not driven by poverty, nor attracted by any immediate prospect of large profits. By the standards of Kenya, they had been fortunate in their search for employment, and were earning more in their last jobs than they took from their businesses in the first few years. Compared with most men of their ages, they had typically more schooling and found better paid, more secure work—as craftsmen, teachers, clerks, soldiers, policemen. Most of them, too, had bought or inherited a few acres of farmland. In the adult population at large about two-thirds of all men were simply peasant farmers, and only 6 per cent had skilled jobs: but three-quarters of the businessmen had given up skilled employment to start their own enterprises. Why should they have taken such risks, of which they were well aware, for very uncertain returns and at the sacrifice of their security?

The answer seems to lie in the frame of reference by which they set their ambitions. In practice, they did not compare themselves with this average, and rest content with their jobs: they compared themselves with the political and administrative élite, and felt deeply frustrated. From the confidence they had inspired in their employers, the way they discussed their business problems, their command of language and the skills they taught themselves, they seemed exceptionally able and energetic men. Many of them, too, had fought hard for Independence. Most were Kikuyu, and half of these had been imprisoned—sometimes for years—for their part in organising the struggle against the colonial regime. Yet once Independence had been achieved, they lacked the educational

qualifications for a role in society that satisfied their ambitions.
Unlike the senior civil servants or political leaders with whom
they identified, they were debarred from responsible and inter-
esting work:

> If they had been more educated, their prospects of
> employment would not have seemed so unsatisfying: in
> more senior jobs, they might have found a sense of impor-
> tance in their work. But the career structure of Kenya is
> closely related to educational attainment, and they lacked
> the formal qualifications which would have entitled them to
> promotion above subordinate posts in the occupational hier-
> archy. This was the underlying cause of their frustration.
> The businessmen had more schooling than most—enough,
> perhaps, to give them a sense of their abilities—but not
> enough to open the way to influential positions. Three-
> quarters had never gone further than primary school, and
> half the rest had not continued their education long enough
> to achieve school certificate standard. Poverty, the disrup-
> tions of the Emergency years, ill-health or their parents'
> indifference had thwarted their educational chances. . .
> Thus the businessmen were excluded from careers which
> might have satisfied their desire to do something important
> and influential in their own eyes. (Marris and Somerset
> 1971, p. 65.)

They therefore defined the aims of business in terms of these
frustrated aspirations. It was not simply a way of making
money, but a means of furthering economic development and
national independence, as crucial and deserving of respect as
government itself. Four-fifths of the businessmen said they
would still prefer business, even if employment paid them better. They saw themselves, like senior civil servants and political
leaders, as builders of the nation. Although their enterprises
were still small, and they were resigned to the low prestige with
which business was conventionally regarded, they dreamt of
mass-production assembly lines, hotel complexes, national distribution agencies, whose contribution would one day be
recognised as equally important. Lacking the education for a
role in development policy, they turned to business as an
expression of economic patriotism—a challenge to the commercial and industrial domination of Kenya by aliens, a source

of employment for the thousands out of work. They transmuted African nationalism into African capitalism, still pursuing the ideals with which they grew up, and still profoundly influenced by the example of the educated élite, whose sophistication and status were the embodiment of modernisation they sought to emulate.

Thus the frustrations which gave rise to their entrepreneurial initiative represented a denial of their self-image. They could not realise themselves in jobs whose limitations they lacked the educational qualifications to escape. Unless they could find a new form of activity to embody their aspirations, they could only look forward to failure in their own eyes. But the aspirations themselves were fundamentally conventional. They were trying to hold on to the ambitions which had governed their lives. It seems to me that much innovation can be understood in these terms—as a means of protecting oneself against a prospective frustration of purposes that make life meaningful.

Until now, the discussion has turned on the loss of relationships which had already existed. But we organise our purposes as much about hopes for the future as about our present life, sometimes identifying with what we will become more meaningfully than with what we are. To fail a crucial examination, miss a coveted job, to be brought up to a position which the world no longer provides may all threaten the purposes and expectations about which the meaning of life has been constructed. They defeat assumptions about the future which have already become crucial to our present identity. In such a situation people suffer a loss of identity, at least in prospect, even though the sense of bereavement may come from a gradual recognition of failure, rather than any definable event. Once someone has set his heart on an attachment, a role in life, disappointment will arouse grief, though they may never have been within grasp. The crisis is more superficial than in bereavement, since a prospective attachment has not yet gathered to it all the habits and secondary purposes whose futility continually reminds a mourner of his loss. But being so vulnerable to disappointment, we beware of setting out expectations too high, adjusting our self-image to our sense of the likely place for us in the world. At the same time, the more resourceful we are the more we can manipulate the future to confirm this image.[1]

Thus the African entrepreneurs turned to business as a way of retrieving their sense of identity from an unpromising impasse. Though the activity itself, with the sophistication they attempted, was foreign to African experience, the purposes it represented for them sustained a greater continuity with the political involvement of their past, with their abortive struggles to complete their education or to retrieve the dispossession of their family's land than a humdrum, if respectable job. The means were new, but the ultimate achievement was to fulfil familiar ideals. At the same time, if business was to compensate for exclusion from the senior civil service and political leadership, it would have to repudiate models of organisation which did not fit this image. The businessmen made a sharp break with both African traditions of economic management, and with the pattern of Asian businesses they sought to rival and replace. They therefore faced great difficulty in organising working relationships compatible with their ideals.

THE DILEMMA OF INNOVATIVE ORGANISATION

Even though the impulse behind entrepreneurship may be fundamentally conservative, it none the less imposes an unfamiliar

---

[1] As Murray Parkes says (1971, p. 104):

A man is tied to his assumptive world. By learning to recognise and act appropriately within his expectable environment a man makes a life space his own . . . the assumptive world not only contains a model of the world as it is . . . it also contains models of the world as it might be (these models may represent probable situations, ideal situations or dreaded situations). Models of the world as it might be are used as a rehearsal ground for actions appropriate to these worlds. The bride-to-be rehearses in her mind the world she hopes to create, she furnishes her home and peoples it with children. It may be almost as hard for her to give up models such as these as to give up objects which actually exist. Hence the girl who has planned for a marriage loses something very important if she is jilted. The change which she has to cope with is a change in her own assumptive world.

way of going about affairs. The African businessmen could not escape the characteristic dilemma of change: how to break habitual conceptions of organisation without destroying the predictability of relationships. They knew what they wanted to make of their enterprises, and they knew what principles of organisation best expressed these ideals, but they had still to formulate them so that their employees, customers and financial backers could also understand and respect them. Hence they needed to reinterpret, rather than repudiate the mutual expectations of behaviour that people were used to. In practice, they tried to escape this dilemma by controlling everything themselves, and this reaction to insecurity was ultimately self-defeating. Thus they partly failed to formulate in their working relationships the continuity which entrepreneurship represented in their own careers.

In the past, African businesses—restricted to petty shopkeeping, bars, carpentry, blacksmithing and repair work —had been seen chiefly as a means of supplementing farm incomes, rather than as a primary career. They were tied to the network of mutual obligations which sustained agricultural society, for the most part a peripheral and subordinate form of livelihood. By contrast, the entrepreneurs we studied characteristically segregated their enterprises from family or community claims as a matter of principle. They recruited employees for their competence and reliability alone, without regard for kinship or tribal affinity. They set fixed prices for all customers alike, and offered credit only to those with financial credentials, resisting favouritism to shareholders, partners or friends. They conceived business as an autonomous system of relationships, governed exclusively by considerations of efficiency, drawing a self-conscious distinction between their role as business manager and their role within the family. Some would refuse to discuss family affairs or requests for help at their place of business: rather than pass a gift across the counter, they would lend money at home out of their personal income, so that the suppliant could make his purchase in the shop like any other customer. Thus they symbolised a differentiation of roles, and a divorce of economic principles from the principles appropriate to other social relationships, incongruous with African traditions. They did not believe these traditions could any longer offer them useful guidance.

In this they were also rejecting the example of the Indian firms with which they competed. These were family enterprises, whose success rested on the exploitation of cheap family labour, and a network of parochial kin and community ties. African businessmen repudiated the Indian model, partly because African traditions of kinship did not adapt well to business co-operation, and their experience with relatives had often proved embarrassing and unproductive. But they also identified more closely with European culture, whose values were much more familiar to them from school, church, working with European employers or dealing with colonial administrators. The traditions of the bazaar, with its bargaining and deviousness, its tight, narrow loyalties and ruthless competition, were by contrast alien and threatening. Nor did Asian business seem to represent ideals of modernisation and national development. Mistrust and misunderstanding of Asian communities, merging with resentment against their principal competitors, drove African businessmen all the more insistently towards an ideal of impersonal, rational, contractual organisation, which they took to represent modern European practice.

Thus, because they identified with the governing élite, and saw themselves as pioneers of modern commercial and industrial enterprises, they went for principles of management more appropriate to a large bureaucratic corporation than a garage, a dry-cleaning plant, or local wholesale distribution. They believed a businessman should be as immune from extraneous community pressures as an ideally impartial civil servant; as dedicated to national, rather than family or tribal purposes, as an ideally patriotic politician. Certainly, there were practical reasons for repudiating claims of kinship: but these reasons were reinforced by the frame of reference in which they sought to define their enterprises.

In practice, no pattern of business could develop on such wholly autonomous and impersonal principles of rational efficiency. African customers expected credit on casual terms, African shareholders expected privileges. Employees were unused to strictly contractual relationships between Africans, and often stole, came late or stayed away without much sense of obligation or remorse. Kinsfolk resented rebuffs to family claims on the business, easy-going friends resented the tight-fisted puritanism which refused to pay out the takings on drink and women. No one shared the businessman's view of his enterprise as a patriotic endeavour whose interests deserved respect, nor understood his insistence on strict dealing. He seemed to own more than most people, with his workshop or well-stocked shelves, his truck or machines, and to be keeping it selfishly to himself. At the same time, as an African newcomer with little experience, he was scarcely integrated with the financial and distributive network which, in European and Asian hands, still dominated the commercial and industrial economy. He lacked the shared conventions, the mutual acquaintances and points of social contact, or the general knowledge to manipulate economic opportunities easily. Both the internal and external relationships of his business were handicapped by lack of mutual confidence. Caught between the traditions of African society, which provided no precedents for paid employment or impersonal contract, and a colonial legacy of commercial and industrial development from which Africans had been deliberately excluded, the entrepreneurs found themselves in limbo.

They therefore tended to withdraw into a suspicious self-reliance. Unable to trust in any established tradition of business relationships, they relied on close personal supervision, delegating little responsibility and watching even their partners with a wary eye. They sought to control their circumstances by concentrating the initiative entirely in their own hands. But this defeated their ambition for large-scale modern enterprises.

If they trusted no one, and supervised everything themselves, they could not expand beyond the limits of face to face control. So while they complained of lack of capital to create the ambitious enterprises of their dreams, they invested their profits in a diversity of minor ventures, each small enough to oversee. This proliferation of interests scattered their attention, and was probably harder to control than a single more substantial concern. But it evaded the insecurity of delegating responsibility, since they hoped to keep their assistants in these sub-

sidiary ventures under close personal control. Thus their
principles of organisation were, in the long run, self-defeating:
impersonal, businesslike efficiency led to hectic personal supervision of an inconsequent scatter of unrelated investments, undermining their progress towards importance in the economy.
They were torn between visions of modern industry, a role of
national economic leadership, and the parochial status of own-
ing the largest butcher's shop in their native township, the
traditional security of a prosperous family farm. Only a few
committed themselves single-mindedly to a career in modern
business and concentrated their talents.

Thus the African businessmen's situation contained tensions
which reproduced more benignly the irresolution of bereavement. The impulse behind their entrepreneurial initiative was
fundamentally conservative—a search for means to reassert
the frustrated aspirations with which they identified the purpose of their lives. But they were also the victims of their own
initiative, as they struggled to restore a predictable pattern of
relationships. They spoke nostalgically of the world of their
forefathers, where people honoured their engagements. But the
ambitions which shaped their business ideals belonged in a
modern African commercial economy as yet scarcely established. Caught between past and future, their reactions were
characteristically ambivalent. For most of them, land still held
a profound, almost mystical meaning, as the life blood of the
family, the ultimate assurance of continuity: and they felt at
ease with the small trading with which prosperous farmers had
always been associated. So they diverted scarce resources from
the enterprises which might achieve their modernising ideals to
familiar African investments which dissipated their profits and
their energies. The strain showed in the anxieties of control, as
they worried restlessly about the opportunities they might have
overlooked, the tasks forgotten, mistrustful of their subordi-
nates and their Asian suppliers. They had the compelling
vitality of men free to be themselves, but they slept badly.

They tried to dominate these anxieties by asserting a personal command corresponding to the self-sufficiency of their
ambitions. The desire for complete autonomy seems a natural
temptation of innovators. Absolute power gives the illusion of

absolute certainty: if everything depends on you, nothing will happen which you have not foreseen. But in any enterprise involving widespreading relationships, it can only be self-defeating: the innovation cannot be assimilated unless its meaning is shared. Others besides the innovator himself must be able to find the thread of continuity in the novelty he imposes. The businessmen needed to evolve relationships of trust and mutual understanding which would once again merge economic life with the enclosing network of social obligations and personal loyalties. Such an evolution depended upon a synthesis between African experience and competitive modern management which had still to work itself out. Like the tribal associations we discussed earlier, the businesses were transitional institutions, which could only succeed by mediating between past and future conceptions of social organisation as yet unreconciled. If the businessmen could not tolerate the ambiguity of organisation that this implied, and tried to resolve it by personal control, they internalised tensions which drove them into contradictory investments and defeated their long-term hopes. Not that they were always unsuccessful, in a small way. But only a few had begun to see the underlying managerial problems they would have to solve, if they were to realise their ultimate ambitions.

The experience of these Kenya entrepreneurs shows how voluntary change can still involve the innovator in a struggle to retrieve a meaningful structure of relationships, comparable with the working out of grief. The colonial history which influenced their ideal of business, and the traditions of African leadership made it particularly difficult to evolve an intermediate form of management. In other settings, entrepreneurial groups have more easily adapted familiar conceptions of kinship or social obligation to the organisation of business. But the analysis of the motive behind the African businessmen's ventures can, I think, be applied to many examples of innovation. The innovator is seeking to confirm his identity, to find new means to realise an established self-image. The rewards he looks for may be ultimately conventional, but he is denied conventional access to them. Rather than submit to the loss of his sense of the meaning of his life, he reinterprets the opportunities that lie in his way.

INNOVATION AS A REACTION TO FRUSTRATION

This interplay of frustration and compensation seems often to explain why entrepreneurs appear. The Samurai of Japan, as Everett Hagen argues (1964, ch. 14), turned to business to recover the purpose and prestige they had lost in the disintegration of feudal society. Clifford Geertz (1963) has shown how, similarly, the Balinese aristocracy exploited old feudal ties to create new large-scale commercial organisations, after Dutch rule and the populist regime which followed had deprived them of political authority. Nonconformist religious groups, too, such as the Quakers or the Jews, have found in business a means to compensate for their alienation from political rights. Some entrepreneurial minorities, like the Indians in East Africa, the Chinese in South East Asia, the Jews, have been at a disadvantage both because of their religion, and because they represent a mistrusted immigrant culture. All these groups have in common, first, a sense of superiority, derived from pride in their class, their ethnic culture or their faith, which will not bow to disparagement or disregard; second, a sense of frustration, because this superiority cannot find recognition through conventional careers; and third, talent, contacts and access to capital, which enable them to create new kinds of organisation.

In each of these instances, the challenge to established orthodoxy was determined by the social position of the innovators. The East African Indians, disqualified from senior positions in the colonial administration and debarred by law from buying farmland, had no choice but to pioneer the unexploited opportunities for commerce and industry, and create the townships of East Africa. The aristocracy of Bali or Japan could not retrieve the feudal society from which they derived their sense of worth. Conversely, innovators are less likely to appear in any group whose access to conventional opportunities conforms to their expectations. Nor can people innovate, whatever the frustrations, if they cannot command resources. Thus entrepreneurship seems to depend on a delicate balance of handicap and potential advantage.

Such an explanation does not, of course, account for every case. Rebels are made, too, by more idiosyncratic accidents of growing up—quarrels with parents, illness, a change in family fortunes. Nonconformity becomes a defining principle of their identity, and they attack conventional society as much out of habit as others defend it. But here again, the innovator is driven by a self-protective impulse: he changes the world, so as not to have to change himself. He seeks out the situations which will confirm his self-image. For instance, Elting Morison has written a detailed account of the introduction of a new technique of naval warfare in terms of the influence of natural rebels. He concludes (1964, pp. 39–40):

> A primary source of conflict and tensions in our case study appears to lie in this great word I have used so often in the summary, the word 'identification'. It cannot have escaped notice that some men identified themselves with their crea-tions—sights, gun, gear, and so forth—and thus obtained a presumed satisfaction from the thing itself, a satisfaction that prevented them from thinking too closely on either the use or the defects of the thing; that others identified them-selves with a settled way of life they had inherited or ac-cepted with minor modification and thus found their satis-faction in attempting to maintain that way of life unchanged; and that still others identified themselves as rebellious spirits, men of the insurgent cast of mind, and thus obtained a satisfaction from the act of revolt itself.[1]

This line of argument suggests how, in general, innovation and conservatism may be related. Most people learn to see themselves in terms of the opportunities familiar to their situa-tion—even at the cost of gross self-disparagement. The harshest function of education is to prepare children realis-tically for their life-chances, and I will come back to this later. But for some, self-image and opportunity are at odds. A social class whose power and privileges are declining may transmit to its children a revised sense of their chances only after a lag

[1] There is an obvious risk of tautology in the final point. But I think it can be stated in a way which is not merely a matter of definition, if the circumstances which lead someone to identify with rebellion can be described independently of the act of rebelling.

even of generations. Race or religion may debar people from
jobs or political status, without incorporating these handicaps,
in the sense in which society intends them, in the way the victims of discrimination see themselves. Or the openness of an
educational system may encourage higher aspirations than it
can satisfy. Such disparities will provoke the symptoms of grief
—apathy, withdrawal, random hostility and guilt. But it may
also set people in search of unconventional ways to realise
their self-image, if they have access to resources. The source of
their frustration can become a potential asset, once they turn
aside from the established structure of opportunity. The solidarity of a religious or racial minority, the deference accorded
an aristocratic family and its network of traditional alliances,
the skills which have proved vocationally redundant, may then
be turned to account.

The frustration which drives people towards innovation may
arise from all kinds of sources; and the activity in which it
finds release may be largely a matter of accident. The complex
of circumstances which generate an entrepreneurial initiative
converge from diverse origins—migration, pressure of population, religious movements, access to resources, new lines of
transportation, inventions, markets, political upset—and each
of these in turn represents an innovation whose origins can be
traced further back. After a generation or two, this initiative
will consolidate into a way of life as predictable as any other.
But I suggest that even at the point in history where people attempt something new, their underlying motive is still, in a
sense, conservative. They displace into original enterprises the
purposes they have learned from the society in which they
grew up, but cannot satisfy within its orthodox framework.
The rewards they hope to win may in themselves be highly
conventional—the successful entrepreneur courts acceptance
by established good society, acquiring its manners and the
trappings of its status. Rebels of genius go to their end ag-
grieved, denied the honorific recognition which in retrospect
seems so trivial. Without this frustration of conventional ambitions, there would be no incentive to undertake the hazardous and unpredictable path of innovation toward the same
ends.

THE ALTERNATIVE EXPLANATIONS TO FRUSTRATION

Explained in these terms, then, entrepreneurship need not qualify the assumption that the conservative impulse is a universal characteristic of human behaviour. Several writers have suggested essentially similar theories. But there are at least two other approaches to consider. Instead of treating entrepreneurship as a displacement of more conventional ambitions —however mediated by historical and social transitions—it can be seen as a function of supply and demand; or as the expression of an intrinsically creative personality.

The first of these alternative explanations assumes only that people will seek to make as much money as they can. Entrepreneurship should then be provoked whenever there seems to be more money to be made by doing something new, so long as the risks appear manageable. If it is not, the trouble lies with imperfections in the market, which frustrate the flow of capital and skills towards their most productive use. Such a model can perhaps account for some entrepreneurial initiatives in a society which already has an aggressive business class with access to risk capital and well-organised markets relatively free from extraneous constraints. But it begs most of the questions. Why are opportunities seized in one economy and not in another with apparently similar potential? If it is because the market is imperfect, the nature of the imperfections has then to be explained, and the argument leads back, I suspect, to conservative influences. Skilled labour is unwilling to migrate, governments legislate against unfamiliar activities, communities demand protection against threatening disruptions of their environment, management cannot assimilate new forms of organisation, businessmen foresee only the kinds of demand and technical developments already allowed for in their experience. Why, too, do some accept the risks of entrepreneurship when others with the same assets shy away? If an enterprise is truly innovative, the risks are likely to be partly unpredictable; all manner of social, political and economic hazards may arise. Hence the perception of risk cannot simply be a matter of calculation, from which any competent businessman would derive the same conclusion, but an aspect of temperament, or the pressures which drive the entrepreneur to take his fortune in his hands.

Against this, it could be argued that however societies differ in their receptivity to change, or men in their blindness, the development of technology overwhelms these disparities, changing the economic setting in ways which must, sooner or later, evoke a response. The underlying cause of change is thus the autonomous evolution of science, whose applied knowledge inexorably alters the value of resources and the nature of demands. If this is true, it is still compatible with a conservative impulse, for the pursuit of knowledge and its applications need not be perceived as threatening to the established way of life: it will be directed, for the most part, to familiar purposes. Once its disruptive implications become apparent it will then be resisted—though by then resistance is too late. The next chapter considers changes of this kind, where the evolution of familiar purposes leads to situations which are no longer familiar, and the structure of meanings becomes threatened. Here I only want to raise the question of whether, after all, technological developments are in themselves fundamental causes of change. The roads, bridges, canals and railways, the enclosures and agricultural reforms which set the conditions of Britain's industrial revolution, for instance, were not made in response to newly discovered techniques. The techniques were improvised as difficulties arose. Brindley, the genius of canal engineering, was a wheelwright who never learned to read and write fluently; he resolved the formidable problems of the Manchester Ship Canal by taking to his bed for days of solitary meditation. The first railways were prepared to use horse-drawn wagons, and the development of a reliable steam locomotive followed. The transformation of lowland Scotland into prosperous farmland depended as much as anything on solid roads, whose original purpose was military repression. Great works of engineering were stimulated by need, created without text-book or precedent by craftsmen of genius, who discovered their principles as they went along. (See, for instance, Smiles, 1862.) Conversely, technical discoveries made before their times have been neglected, and masterpieces of engineering left to rust.

But if explanations which discount social or psychological

differences seem implausible, the process of differentiation need not perhaps involve frustration. Entrepreneurship may be an expression of personality, independent of any thwarting of more conventional ambitions. There are, I think, essentially two possible forms of this argument: one, more sociological, appeals to the influence of character training, the other assumes that the disposition is innate.

In his famous essay, 'The protestant ethic and the spirit of capitalism', Max Weber related entrepreneurship to religious values, and David McClelland has developed this line of enquiry into a more general thesis about the origins of entrepreneurial drive. He conceives a need for achievement as an attribute of personality, inculcated by the values a child assimilates and the pattern of parental care. These values resemble the Protestant ethic, as Max Weber described it, though they are not peculiar to the tradition of the Reformation—sense of vocation, concern with worldly success, thrift and hard work, contempt for luxury and ostentation, responsiveness to challenges of reasonable risk. The appearance or adoption of such values could still be attributed to social frustrations. The innovator rationalises a sense of exclusion from the conventional rewards by identifying with a nonconformist faith: or may endorse values simply because they are in practice, necessary to success in business. The Kenyan businessmen we studied—who believed in hard work, thrift, sobriety, plain dealing and a 'bold heart of risk'—seemed to justify their ethical principles by such pragmatic logic. Or, as Everett Hagen suggests, a subtler process of loss and reaction may, over generations, transform the values of a disinherited class. Entrepreneurship, then, may both validate and be validated by new ethics of behaviour. But is it conceivable that a value system itself, by the character it forms, should be an autonomous cause of innovation?

A system of values, by its nature, offers a stable frame of reference by which to interpret events. Wherever it claims to apply, it assigns a consistent ethical meaning. But a set of principles can only be applied to regular happenings, since their interpretation depends upon recognising the category into which events fall, and this recognition rests in turn on assimilating the present to past experience. It must be predictable what good behaviour should be: how otherwise can its virtue be foretold or recommended? The social ideal may value change and innovation for their own sakes, but novelty, too, must then be perceivable as a regular event. Underlying the novelty is a deeper recognition of its familiar aspect. A society which values risk-taking, individualism, creativity, will provide means to contain them within its structure: but the emphasis on these values then serves to preserve that structure. Corporations may welcome ambitious young executives with original ideas, but the contribution they are expected to make lies within narrow boundaries of assumed purpose and organisational habits. Innovation becomes routinised as good business practice and ceases, in any fundamental way, to innovate. It can only be conceived as good so long as it conforms to expectations: once it oversteps these limits it becomes 'irresponsible' or 'not constructive'. Hence the inculcation of entrepreneurial values would not spontaneously lead anyone to be creative in a manner unforeseen by their training, especially as social rewards will only be apparent in the conventionally approved setting. In this sense, the values are as conservative as any other. The displacement of aspirations into activities which have not before been thought to embody them still needs explanation. The prevailing values of a social group may help to account for the flexibility and imagination with which a career is followed: they cannot in themselves explain divergence from recognised careers.

Suppose, however, that the innovative temperament is innate, or formed by childhood circumstances independent of the prevalent ideology, such as warmth of maternal affection, or the balance of parental control. A class of school children from broadly similar social backgrounds varies as much in creativity as in intelligence, and these disparities—in so far as they are measurable—seem to reflect underlying differences of personality. Some children are consistently more humorous, more wide-ranging in their association of ideas, more divergent in their thinking than others, and they are attracted towards different careers. Since these differences appear in relatively homogeneous populations, they cannot be in any crude or obvious way the outcome of their culture. They are perhaps partly innate, and partly engendered by the manner in which their most intimate relationships have mediated their understanding of their culture. Are entrepreneurs, then, simply extreme personalities, who possess a more insistent, dominant creative impulse than most of us? Joseph Schumpeter, for instance, who first emphasised the role of entrepreneurs in economic theory, endowed them with an atavistic will to power, an intuitive insight, which he did not seek to attribute to any social circumstances.

Since, in fact, entrepreneurs do not appear randomly at all times and places, there must at least be social and economic factors which can stifle creativity. My question, though, is whether the creative impulse may itself account for social innovation, irrespective of any frustration of conventional ambitions. It seems to me unlikely, because if it is natural to be creative, and a society does not deliberately suppress the impulse, a conventional place for it will be established within the social structure. Explaining entrepreneurship by intrinsic abilities must, I think, lead to the same objection as an explanation in terms of values. If entrepreneurial behaviour is compatible with conventional expectations, it is no longer radically innovative. But if it is incompatible, no one would surely undertake so uncertain and stressful endeavour unless they were excluded from easier ways of realising themselves.

The argument reflects the distinction between growth and loss which I outlined in the first chapter. Changes which spring from the development of new skills are not intrinsically disruptive, because they need not involve a break with what has already been learned. So, for instance, a worker in a dry cleaning firm who decides to start his own dry cleaning business can be seen as extending his skills. He may at times become discouraged and perplexed, since learning is often difficult, tempting retreat to more secure and familiar routines. But I do not think that such a career needs to be explained as a reaction to some fundamental frustration of ambitions. It is natural to become restless and dissatisfied with accomplishments which come too easily. Nor would I describe it as entrepreneurship. The African businessmen were not entrepreneurs because they undertook to extend their skills, but because they were seeking to create a new pattern of behaviour. There had never been African businessmen of any consequence before, at least since colonial times. There were no models of behaviour they could copy, since neither European nor Asian patterns of business were viable when translated into relationships between Africans. For an African, starting a substantial business involved a pervasive insecurity of relationships—a willingness to repudiate conventional expectations of kinsfolk, of tribal loyalty and racial or class deference. I do not think people would launch themselves into circumstances so threatening to their sense of identity, unless that sense was already threatened by more profound frustrations. Education would have satisfied their vocational aspirations more reliably and predictably, and they turned to business because educational chances were denied them. Hence I would not expect entrepreneurial ventures to arise commonly amongst groups to whom conventional opportunities of extending their skills are open, however talented they are: nor amongst those who have never learned to expect more than the life chances common to their class.

These interpretations of entrepreneurial initiative are only irreconcilable, however, so long as they are single-mindedly followed. Each illuminates a different aspect of the problem. The African businessmen we studied were certainly inhibited by imperfections of the market—ignorance, racial and cultural prejudices and mistrust constrained their freedom of action, and the chances for any particular business could be predicted more confidently from the nature of its market and the strength of competition than from any other factor. The businessmen identified with a Protestant ethic which, in part, rationalised good business practice; but which also reflected their missionary schooling, and the individualist, competitive traditions of their tribe. They were also, I think, exceptionally creative: they would not otherwise have been so frustrated by the jobs to which their talents had been confined. But neither the opportunities of the market, nor their principles, nor their abilities would, I believe, have led them to abandon secure jobs and plunge into hazardous enterprises, for which there were few precedents in African experience, unless they had also felt that their lives would otherwise be robbed of meaning.

The argument can be generalised to any situation where people deliberately initiate changes which upset the predictability of their lives. They must, I think, foresee some more profound threat to the realisation of their essential purposes, which impels them to withstand the anxieties of breaking out. They repudiate the security of a structure of relationships they understand, so as not to lose the more fundamental attachments which make their lives meaningful. But though what they give up matters less to them, they still confront the struggle to retrieve the continuity of learning—as the African businessmen had somehow to reformulate their sense of kinship, of the meaning of land and the traditions of an African community within the context of a business career. The strains and ambiguities of this struggle continually threatened to undermine their endeavours. The extent to which we are prepared to disrupt the continuity of our lives must, I think, depend on how radically misdirected we perceive our present set of behaviour to be. We are driven to innovate by the incompatibility of present life with our self-conception, rather than by its intrinsic disadvantages. Conversely, the more people have incorporated the defeat of their hopes, the more obstinately they will resist attempts to revive them—as the heroine of Tolstoy's *Resurrection* turns in panic to the rationalisations which justify her life as a prostitute, when her penitent seducer offers, years later, to redeem her.

The idea of prospective loss enables us to see why people should seek changes in which they will suffer at least a residual sense of bereavement. But how do they come to face so uncomfortable a disparity between self-conception and their pattern of life? As Tolstoy's story suggests, to identify with circumstance, to formulate even a tragic or cynical view of life rather than acknowledge an unbearable anomaly, is a less demanding reaction. For the most part, we are brought up to conform our purposes and self-image to our life chances, adjusting them continually to the opportunities within our grasp. We learn early how painful it is to be bereft of hopes on which we have set our hearts. Hence I think the sense of frustration, and the innovative reactions it provokes, are related to contradictions and confusions in society itself, which lead people into such an impasse. The next chapter explores these underlying causes of loss and change.

VII
INCOHERENCE AND SOCIAL CHANGE

My explanation of grief implies that it will be evoked, not only by death, but by any profoundly disruptive loss of meaning. So far, I have discussed three kinds of loss, which can be summarised schematically in terms of a simplified model of learned behaviour. In response to an event, that is, we identify it as belonging to a class of events, and then discriminate the best action in the circumstances. This behaviour will break down, first, if there is no best action, whatever the event, because the actor is robbed of essential purpose, as in severe personal bereavement. But, second, it also breaks down if an event cannot be identified, and every attempt to classify it is proved by what follows to have been mistaken. Repeated experience of unintelligible events will tend to undermine confidence in the possibility of discriminating any best action, even where the sense of purpose has not been lost. This gradual, cumulative sense of bereavement has, I think, shadowed the African response to European colonisation, evoking institutions which express the ambivalence of grief.

Third, besides the loss of attachments and disintegration of a predictable environment, the meaning of life may be threatened prospectively. Since the best action is only definable in terms of its outcome, situations will arise in which no action seems likely to ensure a future that satisfies the essential purposes of the actor. He or she looks forward to bereavement, and must then either revise purposes to make them compatible with the future, or revise the definition of the situation to suggest other possible actions. Both disrupt the structure of established meanings, but either is likely to be less painful than the bereavement that would otherwise follow. Entrepreneurship represents such a redefinition. It deviates from expected behaviour to retrieve the purposes with which the entrepreneurs have come to identify themselves.

But besides losses which bereave us, now or prospectively, of purposeful relationships on which we depend, there is a fourth kind of loss, which destroys only the meaning of a relationship, not the relationship itself. Behaviour may break down, for instance, when the same event falls into more than one category. There may then no longer be one best action, but two or more which mutually exclude each other, according to how the event is interpreted. This is a different problem from an event whose meaning is obscure; here its meanings are clear but contradictory, because it belongs at once to incompatible systems of learned behaviour. The contradiction arises, for instance, whenever someone has to act in the same situation according to conflicting roles. The more complex the society, the more highly differentiated its structures, the greater the risk that incompatible principles of interpretation will converge upon the same events. Consistency depends upon selective attention to only one aspect of a situation at a time, so as to evade the underlying confusion. We discriminate the best action in a given context, looking at it one way, or the best action looking another way, refusing to recognise their mutual inconsistency: and as time goes by, each principle of interpretation will become more elaborate and entrenched. 'Only connect'—the motto with which E. M. Forster prefaced *Howards End*—is the most universal of all radical slogans. The viability of conventional understanding rests in the refusal to make connections. But the latent contradictions may become open and unmanageable, as the consequences of action play themselves out. We can then no longer put off a revision of our principles: and although nothing has been lost except the ability to segregate aspects of experience, the crisis may be as traumatic as bereavement.

In this chapter, I want to extend the idea of bereavement to these processes of societal change, where the interplay of activities intended to consolidate familiar meanings leads to anomalies and contradictions which cannot in the end be ignored. The illustrations are taken mostly from educational issues, especially in Kenya—to link the discussion to the analysis of the African businessmen. But the most clearly articulated parallel to this cycle of consolidation and disintegration in our conception of social institutions is probably the evolution of science. Scientists follow recognised careers within established institutions, yet the outcome of their activities may be radically disruptive. The evolution of science can, I think, be taken as a model of processes which appear more obscurely in the less structured, diffuse processes of social reform.

THE PROFESSION OF SCIENCE

A career in scientific research is defined by the exploration of the unknown. Even the apprentice work by which a student qualifies for the profession is required to contribute something original to the field. Every scientific paper justifies its publication by the new knowledge it contains. The more significant and profoundly original the finding, the greater the prestige of its discoverer, and the competition to pre-empt credit for these discoveries is intense. Yet, paradoxically, the training for this profession is more conservative, and attracts more conservative students, than studies where the pursuit of original knowledge is less crucial. A science student is expected to absorb, uncritically, a body of received ideas, and then reproduce them. As Thomas Kuhn writes (1970, pp. 345–6):

> The single most striking feature of this education is that, to an extent totally unknown in other creative fields, it is conducted entirely through textbooks. Typically, the undergraduate *and* graduate student of chemistry, physics, astronomy, geology or biology acquires the substance of his field from books written especially for students. Until he is ready, or very nearly ready, to commence work on his own dissertation, he is neither asked to attempt trial research projects nor exposed to the immediate products of research done by others, that is, to the professional communications that scientists write for each other. . . . Except in their occasional introductions, science textbooks do not describe the sorts of problems that the professional may be asked to solve and the variety of techniques available for their solution. Rather, these books exhibit concrete problem solutions that the profession has come to accept as paradigms, and they then ask the student, either with a pencil or paper or in the

laboratory, to solve for himself problems very closely related in both method and substance to those through which the textbook or the accompanying lecture has led him.

Thus, in contradiction to all current theory of how best to train creative and original minds, education in the natural sciences 'remains a dogmatic initiation in a pre-established tradition that the student is not equipped to evaluate.' (Ibid.) 'One had to cram all this stuff into one's mind, whether one liked it or not,' Albert Einstein recalled. 'This coercion had such a deterring effect that after I passed the final examination, I found the consideration of any scientific problems distasteful for an entire year.' (Quoted in Parlett, 1970, p. 281.)

Understandably, science seems to attract, and perhaps to mould, more students whose bias is conformist than do arts subjects. Their habit of thought is more close-reasoning, but narrower and more conventional, less playful. The rigidity of the training, its lack of stimulus to creative ideas, seems to reinforce a disposition towards a secure, uncontroversial intellectual framework. 'The attraction that sixth-form science holds for the convergent type of boy now becomes clearer. At this level, science involves no human considerations, little or no controversy, and the assumption that every problem has one correct solution,' writes Liam Hudson. He adds, 'The practical dangers are not only that science may recruit boys who are narrow and inflexible: but, having recruited them, may inadvertently reinforce emotional defenses which unsuit them for original research.' (Hudson, 1970, pp. 302–3.) Yet this educational tradition, whose appeal must surely have always had these implications, has been abundantly productive of original research.

All this suggests that the pursuit of science is, in itself, an expression of the conservative impulse—a search for cognitive structures durable enough to assimilate and accommodate to any event without substantial modification. It represents certainties: the assertion of regularity, whose laws are connected by chains of incontrovertible behaviour. It is, or was, possible to pursue scientific research in isolation from all the moral, political or social issues which trouble the security of our sense of identity. Yet important discoveries do not seem to come only, or even characteristically, from rebels against this orthodoxy. New fields of enquiry may be opened by scientific entrepreneurs, frustrated in conventional research opportunities by the overcrowding of the profession. Divergent thinkers unable to conform to the routines of academic performance may strike out on their own. But originality does not depend on revolt: it arises from the very attempt to consolidate the tradition.

Trained scientists do not usually set out on their careers expecting to overthrow the established theories and findings of their field. As Kuhn says (op. cit., p. 350):

> In pure or basic science . . . the characteristic problems are almost always repetitions, with minor modifications, of problems that have been undertaken and partially resolved before. For example, much of the research undertaken within a scientific tradition is an attempt to adjust existing theory or existing observation in order to bring the two into closer and closer agreement. . . . The development of chemical thermodynamics or the continuing attempts to unravel organic structure illustrate another type—the extension of existing theory to areas that it is expected to cover but in which it has never before been tried. In addition, to mention a third common sort of research problem, many scientists constantly collect the concrete data . . . required for the application and extension of existing theory. These are normal research projects in the basic sciences, and they represent the sorts of work on which all scientists, even the greatest, spend most of their professional lives and on which many spend all.

Clearly, such research only makes sense, so long as received ideas are taken for granted. 'Under normal conditions the research scientist is not an innovator but a solver of puzzles, and the puzzles upon which he concentrates are just those which he believes can be both stated and solved within the existing scientific tradition.' (Ibid., p. 351.) But it follows, just because research topics are framed within the prevailing analytic assumptions, and chosen to confirm and elaborate them, that, if the problem cannot after all be solved on these assumptions, there must be something fundamentally wrong.

Hence the interdependence of conservatism and innovation in the evolution of science. The consolidation of a given structure of meaning is carried forward single-mindedly, on the assumption that it can interpret any event within its field of application, and apparent discrepancies are due to faulty observation or mistaken inference. Only the most insistent and obstinately unintelligible disparities between theory and events can shake the tradition. But once the disparities are acknowledged their implications are inescapable, given the assumptions of the tradition itself, as Kuhn points out (ibid., p. 351):

> At least for the scientific community as a whole, work within a well-defined and deeply-ingrained tradition seems more productive of tradition-shattering novelties than work in which no similar convergent standards are involved. . . . No other sort of work is nearly so well suited to isolate for continuing and concentrated attention those loci of trouble or causes of crisis upon whose recognition the most fundamental advances in basic science depend.

If this is so, you would expect the breakdown of established theory to become apparent to many researchers at about the same time, as irrefutable objections are repeatedly noticed. Correspondingly, the discovery of a new theory which resolves the problem is likely to occur to more than one investigator. However brilliant the solution, it derives from the facts and intellectual background shared by the community of scientists, and has probably been prefigured in earlier work whose implications had not been fully recognised before. The tradition contains the latent discordance which will eventually destroy it; but the nature of the discordance will also mark the direction in which the solution lies. Hence the attribution of scientific discovery to an individual genius is more a matter of timing than unique insight—often enough a race between rivals, where the winner outdistances the field by a few weeks, or scarcely even twenty-four hours. The leaders watch each other anxiously, deploying the pre-emptive tactics at their command to disarm the competition—sealed envelopes of preliminary findings, deposited with learned societies; private letters reporting progress; publications; while an intelligence network of sympathetic colleagues warns them where they risk being forestalled. Thus the profession itself recognises that the path of discovery is rarely travelled alone: even the most brilliant look nervously over their shoulders, or worse, fear to come upon the retreating figure of a distinguished colleague round the next bend. Robert Merton has estimated that—taking the known cases where discoveries have been independently made, and those where lines of enquiry have been abandoned or publication forestalled because a rival was there first—multiple discoveries are the rule in science (Merton, 1970, p. 76):

> A great variety of evidence—I have here set out only ten related kinds—testifies, then, to the hypothesis that once science has become institutionalised and significant numbers of men are at work on scientific investigation, the same discoveries will be made independently more than once, and that singletons can be conceived as forestalled multiples.

Not that innovations in science are achieved without imagination. But the imagination works within an intellectual context where, although the most brilliant will make more discoveries, they are unlikely to be entirely alone in any one of them. Conversely, anyone who challenges the orthodoxy before its intellectual drawbacks have become generally apparent risks ridicule, vilification or neglect. Men have been driven to suicide by the obstinacy with which the scientific community rejects evidence contradicting established theory. This aggressive conservatism, which will even libel a colleague's integrity rather than accept his findings, tests the durability of the tradition to its limits. But once its weaknesses have been shown to be fundamental, the impact is overwhelming.

This sketch of the practice of science follows Thomas Kuhn. Since his interpretation is controversial, and most of the criticisms centre upon his conception of the revolutionary transitions, I should discuss these transitions in a little more detail. They are especially important to my present argument, because I want to show how, in general, activities which are seeking to defend a familiar structure of meaning may in the end destroy it. Scientific revolutions, if Kuhn is right, are not the outcome of diffuse, challenging critical speculation, but a response to loss. The familiar habits of thought are disrupted by cumulative anomalies in the observations undertaken to make them more secure; and the disruption is a crisis, an intellectual bereavement, not a normal episode in the continual process of scientific discovery.

But can the distinction between normal scientific work and its revolutionary transitions be sustained? Every valuable enquiry advances the subject in some way, every revolution has theoretical and experimental antecedents. Looked at a little differently, are not the achievements of normal science minor revolutions, and revolutions only major steps in a normal evolution? On this view, the notion of a conservative, normal science is misleading: all scientific work intends to be innovative, and the differences are only of degrees. But this interpretation disregards a qualitative difference between major and minor revisions, corresponding to the difference between grieving and routine adaptation, which seems important. Conversely, if, indeed, the progress of science is constrained by unchallenged assumptions, why should the assumptions ever be overthrown? If at one time the scientific community agrees to treat incompatible evidence as a puzzle to be resolved within the framework of current theory, why at another does it treat such evidence as a crucial refutation? Kuhn has been accused of presenting scientific revolutions as a matter of fashion or mob psychology, a response to social pressure rather than the critical revision of theory by experimental test. Anything so morally repugnant, the critics seem to imply, cannot be a true picture of the noblest of mankind's intellectual endeavours.[1] But a scientific revolution does not become capricious, because it cannot be shown to be logically necessary, in any absolute sense. It can be seen as a response to growing intellectual frustration, which does present itself as a crisis where the whole nature of a scientific tradition may be thrown in doubt. In this,

[1] These criticisms, together with Thomas Kuhn's reply, are set out in Lakatos and Musgrave (1970). Stephen Toulmin's paper, for instance, questions whether the distinction between normal and revolutionary science is valid; John Watkins, Paul Feyerabend and Karl Popper are all worried by the normative implications of Kuhn's thesis. This brief sketch of the controversy does not do it justice, but I hope it is enough to explain the general principles of the argument I wish to apply.

I think, it is not unlike the personal or social crises, where our sense of the meaning of life seems fundamentally threatened by contradictions and inconsistencies we can no longer ignore.

What, then, makes a scientific revolution? Firstly, the intellectual framework to be overthrown is not so much a specific theory, as a direction of enquiry guided by a fundamental metaphor—a way of looking at events in terms of clockwork, or waves or clusters of balls or organisms—which suggests the kind of model to be developed and refined as theory. This framework is associated with a field of observation, with techniques of experiment and interpretation, with a set of scientific habits inculcated by education, enshrined in their most celebrated demonstrations, and reinforced by their theoretical justifications. But the work as a whole—the paradigm of scientific procedure—does not depend on the perfection of the theory: it is justified rather by its success in progressively resolving anomalies, extending the scope of its predictions, uncovering new facts.[1] A scientific tradition is justified by the productivity of its research strategy; and so long as its potential seems unexhausted, inconsistent findings can be left to one side, on the assumption that sooner or later the puzzle can be resolved. In practice, a great many inconsistencies can be resolved, by refining the explanatory metaphor, improving the accuracy of experimental techniques, reinterpreting findings or—less confidently—by adding *ad hoc* explanations. Newtonian physics, again and again, turned apparently anomalous findings into triumphant vindications. So a scientist takes a very great risk in accepting a finding as a crucial refutation of fundamental theory. If he or she has no more promising research strategy to offer in its place, the finding may be simply ignored: it must be a mistake of some kind not worth the diversion of energy to investigate. Or colleagues may take up the challenge, and the chances are that in one way or another they can discredit either the findings or its interpretation. Hence there are rarely rewards for taking such

[1] See Imre Lakatos, 'Methodology of Scientific Research Programmes', in Lakatos and Musgrave (1970), for an interpretation of scientific theory in terms of research strategies. Margaret Masterman's paper in the same book develops the notion of scientific paradigms.

a risk either to the scientist or the subject, and all training discourages it. Yet years later the findings may be recognised as the harbinger of a revolution; and seeing with other eyes, people will say 'how blind they were then'.

Eventually, however, even the most revealing metaphors exhaust their explanatory potential. Anomalies begin to resist every attempt to crack their puzzling inconsistency with theory; or the solving of puzzles turns out to generate new and more difficult problems. The qualifications which save the fundamental assumptions begin to proliferate incoherently. The research programme is then seen to be degenerating, as the guiding principles lead more and more often up blind alleys. Beside this internal confusion, incompatible lines of scientific thought may converge upon the same subject matter, as each expands its scope; and if the same events can be explained in terms of profoundly different metaphors, how can both metaphors be equally true pictures of reality? Once the two research programmes can no longer be segregated, the ambiguity threatens the basic strategy of science, since the underlying theoretical assumptions can no longer be protected from continual debate. Science is forced back towards a preoccupation with its metaphysical foundations: and until it can recover some conventional paradigm of reality in which to put its faith, the profession of science loses confidence in its identity. Applied research may proceed differently, starting from a problem defined independently of theory—such as a cure for cancer. The task then is to relate theory to fact, rather than fact to theory, by a research programme which explores a variety of lines of thought, without being committed to any. But I am concerned here with the intrinsic problems generated by the evolution of a science.

Thus the crises can be distinguished from the normal progress of discovery by the disintegration of the whole structure of interpretation to which a body of work has been assimilated. The distinction can be put in terms of Piaget's two basic principles of adaptation—assimilation and accommodation. Normal events can be assimilated, roughly at least, by the present structure, which then accommodates to features of the event for which its previous experience had not prepared it. But critical events cannot be assimilated at all, until the structure accommodates. This is much more difficult, because the less assimilable events are, the harder to see what kind of accommodation would be successful; and in trying to accommodate, the ability of the structure to grasp events which were formerly assimilable may be undermined. The whole structure is then threatened by radical confusion. Suppose, for instance, a specimen is discovered which does not fit the established system of classification. Normally it can still be placed within the framework of the taxonomy, which accommodates by adding a new class or sub-class. But say it combines features which the taxonomy assumes to be defining qualities of mutually exclusive classes. The specimen cannot then be placed at all. The principles of classification must be revised first, as a whole. Everything that has already been classified has also to be re-examined. The tactic of minimal, incremental accommodation, which normally strengthens the adaptability of the structure, is no longer reliable. The situation is qualitatively different from the normal case, even in a minor revolution. Primitive classifications, which cannot accommodate to anomalies, may treat them as dangers to be avoided and reviled. (See Mary Douglas on 'the abominations of Leviticus' in *Purity and Danger*, 1966.)

The breakdown of interpretative structure is redeemed by imposing a new structure—another way of looking, a different metaphor which will bring with it a new direction of enquiry, new techniques and habits of thought. To perceive this new metaphor is the crucial act of creative imagination. It seems often to come about by importing a pattern of organisation from another field of enquiry, adapting the principles designed to solve quite different sorts of puzzles. (Arthur Koestler gives many examples of this leap of imagination in *The Act of Creation*, 1964.) Thus the resolution of the crisis resembles those teasing party puzzles which are insoluble within the framework of thought they call to mind, but yield easily once you look at them differently, say in three dimensions rather than two, or as a linguistic rather than numerical sequence. This new metaphor may be latent in the old, as a theory is elaborated and qualified. The original image has become distorted into something more closely resembling the new, but the language of analogy has not changed—as if, for instance, one were to represent some aspect of reality as a clockwork, but a self-winding, self-correcting clockwork which is somehow able to regenerate its own parts: at which point it may be much more revealing to think in terms of a plant. The moment of insight, when the connection is intuitively made, seems to precede any detailed articulation of theory: and at the outset, the new line of thought may well present as many unresolved anomalies as the old. But they are of a different nature. Unlike the obstinate difficulties of the older theory, they have yet to show that they are insoluble puzzles.

Thus a scientific revolution grows out of the recalcitrant anomalies and contradictions which beset current thinking, and disillusionment with the promise of its research programme. The revolution itself represents a fundamental shift of perception, a new pattern of organisation which solves some crucial and frustrating problems, stimulates a new line of research, predicts new findings, is simpler, more elegant, and can comprehend most, if not all, the insights of the framework it usurps. And if it is indeed a revolution, its perception must be incommensurable with the old. It cannot be fully translated into the terms of the previous theory, for otherwise it is merely a restatement, not a revolution.

Yet scientists must still judge the risks when they commit themselves to a radically new line of thought. They cannot be sure that its discrepancies with observed events will be reconciled by research, or its predictions consistently fulfilled; nor that the difficulties of the older theory were ultimately insoluble in its own terms. Their judgment is entrepreneurial rather than strictly logical. Just as a businessman sees how a new pattern of organisation might exploit resources more profitably, so a scientist changes the metaphor from a sense that it will be more productive of knowledge. They are justified by the achievements of their strategy, not the logical invulnerability of its conception: and for these achievements to be realised, a scientific community must accept the promise of the new directive as an act of faith. Those who hang back, unconvinced, can only be dismissed as eccentric reactionaries once the strategy has confirmed its promise.

Thus the crises of science represent a breakdown in the structure of meaning, and out of this intellectual bereavement a new structure of interpretation is assembled, more powerful and coherent, by which the continuity of the tradition is restored. Innovation, once again, appears as a means of reintegrating experience and retrieving a sense of its meaning in the face of loss. The revolution is a reformulation, abstracting the essential meaning of past understandings from their original context. But the distinctive quality of the scientific process is the insistent puzzle solving which makes recurrent crises inescapable. The urge to extend and consolidate the implications of theory will sooner or later expose its underlying weakness. Hence it is possible to follow a scientific career in an essentially conservative spirit, while yet hoping that the glory of a radical breakthrough will fall to one's part.

As I shall try to show, a similar evolution of latent inconsistencies betrays our social understanding, and then, too, we are forced to innovate by the consequences of our very attempts to conserve our sense of purpose. But here the crisis is not encapsulated within a tradition whose intellectual resources are uniquely sophisticated and insulated from extraneous anxieties. Although in practice scientific discovery may have far-reaching social implications, research scientists protect themselves by pretending otherwise: the pursuit of knowledge is treated as a self-enclosed system, whose conceivable applications lie beyond their professional responsibility. But in both science and social policy, the way we see the world implies action, a strategy of research or intervention. Unless we commit ourselves to these metaphors of reality we remain impotent, and unlike science, social metaphors involve our crucial emotional attachments and their loss can provoke grief.

INCOHERENCE AND SOCIAL CHANGE

The process of scientific discovery illustrates a crisis in understanding which recurs continually, though far less systematically, in the conventional wisdom of society. I argued in the preceding chapter that entrepreneurial behaviour, as one example of change-seeking, characteristically arises from frustration. But the frustrations which generate entrepreneurship can, I think, themselves be traced to underlying tensions in society. These tensions can in turn be seen to represent fundamental confusions of purpose, an incoherence in the meanings by which we interpret events, continually undermining the stability of our assumptions. If this is so, change itself can be taken as an attempt to consolidate a viable construction of reality more secure from ambiguity and disillusionment, as a new scientific theory tries to overcome the inconsistencies of its forerunner.

So, for instance, the problems of the African businessmen reflected a pervasive tension in Kenya society. The disparity between life chances and the assumptions people came to adopt, about the world and their place in it, were rooted in the ambiguities of colonial rule. Tensions such as these are surely common to most societies, and they are likely to be especially obvious in education, since it is here that expectations are learned. Let me start by exploring them in the Kenya setting.

The sense of an educational mission was crucial to the moral justification of imperial rule. Britain could not impose a government on its colonies blatantly inconsistent with its own political philosophy, without undermining the legitimacy of its intervention. Colonial adventures which contradict the assumptions on which metropolitan society itself bases the right to govern tend to become dangerous political liabilities. At the same time, liberal, democratic colonial government seemed neither feasible nor desirable. European settlement in Kenya and the establishing of an overall administrative structure required the alienation of African pastures, interference with tribal custom, and the imposition—sometimes by force—of an authoritarian bureaucracy. Practice and political principle were reconciled by the concept of guardianship: primitive Africans, rescued from ignorance and Arab slave dealing, would gradually learn to govern themselves under kindly but firm guidance. It was naturally to be a slow process. The colonising power claimed, rather grandly, the experience of two thousand years of civilisation, while African tribes—as the British were never tired of remarking—had not even discovered the wheel. However hypocritical it may seem in retrospect, this colonial philosophy was sincerely believed by many of its administrators, and it implied a commitment to African education. Education has remained the nodal point of tension in African society ever since. Colonial administrators

could not deny education, without repudiating their moral
justification; but they found Africans who spoke English and
imitated European ways pretentious, uppitty and suspect. Men
like Kenyatta, who understood the British political system, and
tried to exploit its parliamentary principles both at home and
abroad, were clearly subversive. Colonial policy was also committed to securing the future of European agriculture, on
which the economy was to base its development, and discouraged, throughout the Depression, commercial farming by Africans. African education was not, therefore, to open access to
either political or economic power in the near future, but only
to subordinate ranks in administration and professions.

Yet in African eyes, education *was* the key to power. The
Kikuyu, able farmers themselves, had been deeply impressed
by European cattle, but their first attempts to keep them failed,
and they realised they had much to learn about European hus-
bandry: so with trade, crops, machines and institutions. European knowledge was evidently very powerful, and Africans
would never recover control over their own destiny until they
had acquired it. They saw this knowledge as inhering in a culture, and resisted well-meaning attempts to adapt school cur-
ricula more realistically to African needs. Whenever European
educators suggested a more relevant syllabus, Africans
suspected a plot to hold them in ignorance. Thus African na-
tionalists came to challenge their colonial rulers in the name of
values which the rulers could neither deny nor honour—education, economic development, Protestant self-determination.
The philosophy of guardianship raised aspirations which
it then had continually to repress.

At the same time, the system of education itself emulated
the traditions of English grammar and public schools, imposing an élitist ideal on the much more egalitarian traditions of
African society. The ambition for education was not, as in Britain, contained by a sense of class boundaries. Education was
the crucial secret of power, which anyone might grasp with
luck and determination, and its rewards were not seen to
depend on scarcity of access. Thus a narrowly academic system of learning, preoccupied with competitive examinations
and suited primarily to the recruiting of an administrative hier-

archy, came to be seen as the universal key to prosperity and status.

Thus both the colonial administration and its African subjects equated power and opportunity with European education. Each then faced a different dilemma. How was the colonial regime to liberalise its government, as more Africans achieved education, without losing control of the situation? In practice, any concessions were bound to be exploited as a lever to wrest further concessions, defeating the ideal of orderly, gradual progress towards self-government on Imperial terms. Yet to repudiate liberal reforms altogether undermined the moral justification of the whole colonial enterprise. For the Africans, the dilemmas were more profound and enduring. The conquest of European knowledge seemed, and I believe still seems, the only way of redeeming the humiliation of colonisation—to prove themselves the equal of their former masters; to achieve success, personally and nationally, in the terms which counted in a world dominated by the industrial powers. Yet so long as this alien frame of reference was accepted, no African nation would ever be master of its own destiny, nor safe from continual reminders of inferiority. The equation of education and power was not simply spurious: but it concealed a fundamental disparity between aspirations and opportunities.

This incongruity gave rise to repeated and increasingly desperate attempts to find a new integration. The Independent Schools movement in the 1930s tried to combine African nationalism and defence of Kikuyu custom with the frustrated demand for European-style education. A generation later, the 'Mau Mau' rebellion stemmed from the same roots—though its attempts at synthesis were more bizarre and naive, as it struggled to bind a rudimentary insurgent parliament and army of liberation with the sanctions of a quasi-traditional oath. On the other side, the colonial administration experimented with a series of constitutions, each designed to concede a measure of democracy without surrendering European control, before it was finally driven to recognise the instability of any political compromise.

Independence resolved the political ambiguity, but the disjunction between educational aspirations and opportunity remained. The movement for 'Harambee' schools, locally ini-

tiated and financed by community subscription, forced on a
reluctant government an expansion of secondary education it
had neither the teachers or resources to sustain, nor the jobs to
reward. Farmers sold their land to buy an education for their
children that was less and less likely to qualify them for a
worthwhile career. The whole pattern of ambition and expend-
iture was still distorted by a misconceived faith in English
schooling rooted in the colonial experience. Both individually
and collectively, the transfer of formal educational opportunities had become confused with the transfer of power. People
built schools and pursued paper qualifications as if these, in
themselves, were the key to prosperity, because the colonial
power had so presented them. It had at once controlled African access to education to maintain its authority, and used the
restriction to justify its continued guardianship.

I have tried to show how entrepreneurship arose out of these
frustrations: many of the businessmen themselves had been involved in both the Independent Schools and the rebellion, and
were still active in promoting local education. But this is only
one reflection of a tension whose implications for change have
many facets. The incongruity could only finally be resolved either by evolving a class structure, wherein most people would
expect only as much education as would maintain them at their
parents' level; or by destroying the educational system as the
arbiter of life-chances. Kenya may be drifting towards the first
and Tanzania reaching for the second. Both outcomes would
disrupt the image which, I believe, most Africans hold of their
society—as classless, open to ambition, and deeply committed,
as a matter of pride, to emulating the achievement of great
powers. And if the issue cannot be resolved in either way, it
must provoke a restless search for compromises and evasions
—new kinds of schools, redefinitions of social ideology, élitist
strategies of containment, the search for status through
unorthodox careers. Yet the impetus behind these innovations
is still a conception of purpose formed by the discoveries and
humiliations of colonisation.

The Independent Schools and the 'Mau Mau', like Ibo tribal
associations, were ambivalent institutions, searching for a synthesis that would relate the past to the future, and give the
present a meaningful purpose. They expressed a sense of iden-

tity lost, as well as hopes for a national identity yet to be realised. This incorporation of unreconciled impulses is, as we have seen, characteristic of mourning institutions. But they were also, like entrepreneurship, reactions to the inherent contradictions of contemporary society—the simultaneous assertion and denial of education as the one legitimate means to power, and the academic formality of that education in a society whose principal needs were technical and agricultural skills.

Thus the disintegration of the colonial ideal was not unlike the progressive degeneration of a scientific paradigm. The original motives for colonisation derived from the commercial and political ambitions of European nationalism, softened by a more humane desire to rescue the people of Africa from slavery and ignorance. The metaphor of guardianship reconciled these motives, justifying authoritarian rule, the implanting of European settlers to pioneer agricultural development, and a network of mission-sponsored schools. Together they were to secure the basis of a gradual evolution towards a prosperous, stable, multi-racial society modelled in the image of a liberal democracy. At the outset, guardianship seemed to represent the true nature of the relationship, for Africans were surely ignorant, and the colonisers believed sincerely enough in their moral purpose. It also set a programme of development, and provided a framework of interpretation by which to predict and evaluate the course of events. But as the metaphor was exploited and extended, its latent weakness was exposed, and the disparity between fact and theory involved more and more precarious rationalisations.

Guardianship implies an identity of interest between guardian and ward: already in the 1920s, it was clear that the Imperial power could not easily reconcile its commitment to European settlement with the principle that African interests were paramount. Guardianship also implies that the ward will come into his inheritance as he matures, but a co-operative devolution of power became impossible once land had been alienated for Europeans. Since the metaphor assumed an identity of interest, colonial administrators could only understand African political opposition as the work of unrepresentative, irresponsible agitators. Their policies became an increasingly frus-

trated search for the 'true' representatives who would validate
their theory, drawing the African majority behind their co-
operative leadership. When the 'Mau Mau' rebellion exposed
the futility of these hopes, the administration was driven to
more far-fetched rationalisations. It took the rituals of oath-
taking at face value, and believed that the rebels were be-
witched by supernatural fears. Hence the suppression of revolt
was guided by a theory of rehabilitation, where forced confes-
sion and the symbolic breaking of the oath were to exorcise the
spell. The theory was only discredited when, in the course of a
crudely mismanaged exercise in rehabilitation, several prisoners were beaten to death, scandalising public opinion in
Britain.

From a British point of view, the dismissal of African na-
tionalists as agitators, the interpretation of rebellion in pathological terms, the devising of interim constitutions, even the
final concession of Independence, can all be seen as a succession of attempts to rescue the viability of the metaphor by
which the colonial experience had been interpreted. And this
conception of colonial relationships was so ingrained in the institutions of society that Africans as well as Europeans accepted it. Political independence did not therefore fundamentally change the paradigm. Kenyans still set their national
ideals at the imitation of contemporary European society, and
still saw their relationship with the great powers as one of
tutelage—though they now had freedom to choose their subjects and their teachers. But the anomalies became more and
more obtrusive. Neither the political institutions, nor the tech-
nologies, nor the educational priorities of rich industrial
democracies fitted well with African needs. The disparity of
wealth between rich nations and poor only grew, while the
disparity between aspirations and opportunities within society
became increasingly unmanageable. The entrepreneurship of
the Kenya businessmen derived from these frustrations. But
behind their exploration of new, less academic careers as
modernisers of society lies a crisis in the meaning of modernisation itself. This crisis was, I believe, latent from the outset
in the whole conception of guardianship. It is now so apparent
that everything it implied—educational structures, patterns of
economic growth, international aid—is thrown in doubt; and

we search for a new metaphor to reinterpret the past and predict the future.

This cracking open of a latent inconsistency is not peculiar to colonial societies. The awkwardness of Kenya's school system, for instance, only dramatised the ambiguity inherent in the educational philosophy of contemporary democracies. Behind the expansion of higher education, the waves of student rebellion, the frustrations of remedial projects in ghetto schools, lies an unresolved contradiction.

THE AMBIVALENCE OF DEMOCRATIC EDUCATION

We understand teaching as the fostering of ability. Ideally, it seeks to cultivate every valuable skill—instrumental, emotional, social or imaginative—a child may be able and want to develop. At the same time, the educational system institutionalises the allocation of vocational opportunities. It must therefore deny most children the chance to acquire skills which only a few can exercise. The contradiction can only be reconciled by assuming that the distribution of talent corresponds to the distribution of opportunities: the number of potential surgeons providentially equals the number society can support in their accustomed style. But this equation can only be given an appearance of reality by a system of competitive examination, which regulates standards of qualification to suit the places. Without gross cynicism, such an examination system is only tolerable so long as people believe that examinations do, indeed, discriminate more or less scarce and valuable talent, directing children benignly towards the occupations in which they can best realise their natural aptitudes. Talent becomes identified with the examination performance which defines it: and examination performance in turn becomes identified with vocational qualification.

This conception of an educational system seems inherently unstable. If education serves to foster ability, it must logically expand in an egalitarian society until every child has the chance to develop any skills he or she can. And if it also allocates job opportunities, it must in turn elaborate its examination system to contain this wealth of new recruits. Since the standards of an existing examination cannot be too radically revised without exposing how arbitrarily independent of needed ability they are, the restriction of opportunity depends on instituting ever higher and higher levels of qualification. As more children graduate from high school, as universities and colleges of higher education multiply, shop-keepers begin to demand a high school diploma from their sales-assistants, executives a university degree from their secretaries, and the professions close their ranks to anyone without post-graduate training. Both the expansion and the counterbalancing restriction are, I suggest, essentially conservative. Each is reinforcing an aspect of the meaning of education deeply ingrained in our thinking. To frustrate a child's talent, or to compromise the competitiveness of excellence are equally abhorrent. Yet the interaction of these principles must eventually reach a crisis. The disparity between the promise of education, the abilities it encourages children to discover in themselves, and the openings to which it leads become more and more glaringly obvious. If teachers in ghetto schools disparage their pupils and deny their talents, they may be unfaithful to their educational ideals, but they acknowledge the poverty of their pupils' vocational chances, reflecting honestly enough the repressive aspect of the educational system. And for this they are regularly attacked by a society that will neither give up its egalitarian ideals, nor translate them into an egalitarian employment policy.

The education of women involves a similar contradiction, leading them towards intellectual and vocational ambitions which neither their opportunities nor their conventional feminine role can satisfy. No incremental adjustment of opportunities or expectations seems likely to resolve these ideological tensions: the underlying hypocrisy only becomes more evident. So radical solutions gain ground. Either education must be restructured, as part of an egalitarian revolution: or the whole egalitarian tradition must be discarded. The revived arguments emphasising inherent differences in intelligence or social expectations are as radical in their implications as those of the Left.

At the same time, as the point of entry into a career becomes further and further postponed, the discrepancy between vocational maturity and any other adult status becomes increasingly unmanageable. At one time, most people started work long before they were grown up. But as higher education expands, as jobs for those without a superior degree become less rewarding, more and more young people will be driven to endure an intellectual adolescence prolonged for several years after they are voting citizens and emotionally adult. Except for the academic élite, the rest will acquire an intellectual sophistication out of all proportion to the occupations they can expect to follow, submitting to an irksome tutelage without much prospect of ever using the skills they acquire by it. If, in their frustration, they demand control over their education as grown men and women, and insist that the subjects of their courses reflect their interests, rather than intellectual competence in fields they are never likely to explore professionally, their revolt seems rational. Yet they still cannot give up the competitive advantage of a formal qualification without endangering their careers: and the validity of these qualifications depends on legitimation by the academic authority they challenge. They want a degree on their own terms, which no professor could grant without a compromise of intellectual integrity. Yet conversely, universities cannot arbitrarily restrict their recruits to the numbers they can place professionally without betraying their liberal traditions of worldly detachment.

I have tried to trace the implications of the way formal education is conceived and instituted, from the frustrations which provoke African entrepreneurship to the pervasive frustrations of colonisation, the ambiguities of African nationalism and the inconsistency underlying the educational philosophy of the colonial power itself. Similar dilemmas trouble many issues of policy. The logic of all our systems of social and economic control belies the doctrine of human equality which ultimately justifies them. However we try to evade the dilemma, an uneasiness remains. We may reformulate equality as equal opportunity, or the rebellious frustration of the unlucky as a pathology, but the anomalies remain. Like the crises in the evolution of science, we reach a point where the underlying assumptions can no longer be saved by reinterpreting awkward evidence within their framework. But because the framework of thought is much looser, the guiding paradigms less clearly articulated, the implications so much more diffuse and personally threatening, the crisis is both less obvious and harder to resolve.

The tensions of such crises provide the impetus for reform. They determine what aspects of society are perceived as crucial problems—for clearly, the prevalence of poverty, delinquency, the denial of rights, are not in themselves problematic, unless they contradict our understanding of what should be. These tensions evoke a reaction which, like grief, swings between irreconcilable impulses in a restless search for resolution. As Martin Rein and I concluded from our study of American anti-poverty programmes (1967, p. 233):

> Confronted by the dilemmas of social choice, reform does not seem most characteristically to search for a balance. Instead, it takes up each of the incompatible principles by turn, and campaigns for it as if no sacrifice of its alternative were entailed. And this seemingly irrational refusal to come to terms with the fundamental dilemma may, after all, be more productive than accommodation. By repudiating whatever balance has been struck, it continually challenges society to explore new ways of meeting the problem. . . . The debate goes round and round, raising the same perennial issues, but the context of argument changes.

Here, I think, the element of fashion also comes into play, accentuating the rearrangement of ideas whose inter-relationship has always been, in part, arbitrary and variable.

The conservatism of society rests, therefore, on insecure foundations. As we follow, step by step, the logic of familiar assumptions, we are led towards new crises where the latent inconsistencies in our interpretations of life become manifest: and every attempt to resolve these crises sets up disruptive repercussions. Since, most often, we learn the meaning of events in specific situations, the principles which come to govern our behaviour in one kind of situation are not necessarily compatible with what we have learned in another. A child learns to stand up for himself at school, but aggressive self-defence is frowned on at home. What is he to do if he encounters his brother as an antagonist in the school playground? To protect the integrity of all he has already learned, he has to invent a new principle, instituting a compromise or assigning the situation to one category or another—family loyalties do not count at school, school conventions are subordinate to family. Either way, he cannot avoid innovation. And the new interpretation, worked out to restore the viability of familiar understandings, may in turn have far-reaching implications for the coherent understanding of other situations. Thus the idea that a brother can only be treated as a brother in certain circumstances plants a distinction between people and roles which will raise again and again thereafter profoundly difficult problems of behaviour.

If the sense we have learned to make of one kind of relationship cannot be translated to another, ambiguities threaten to arise whenever the relationships merge: the same person appears in different roles, or circumstances force separate aspects of life into a common frame of action. We try to escape these ambiguities by rules of avoidance: a judge is excused from trying his friend, an official from the appointment committee before whom his kinsman appears as a candidate. But these rules give rise to further ambiguities: if the principle of impartiality is extended from judge to jury, from friendship to any ground for prejudice, the possibility of a fair trial becomes more and more remote. Once political, class or racial prejudice are raised as legitimate objections, no court of law is unchallengeably neutral. Justice becomes discredited by the very attempt to assert its principles unambiguously. Thus the attempt to clarify and protect our sense of a relationship can lead towards new and troubling inconsistencies at every level of organisation from a marriage to a nation. A society works out the implications of discordant ideals to the point of collision. An organisation may ultimately disintegrate as its constituent roles play out the inherent logic of their self-protective tactics. A marriage draws imperceptibly towards crisis by a series of adjustments each intended to reaffirm its meaning. As we try to make what we understand more secure, we blunder against contradictions we did not foresee, as the reinforcement of one aspect of our sense of life knocks another precariously off balance.

In this way situations akin to bereavement arise, although nothing has been lost except the ability to segregate incompatible aspects of our interpretation of the social environment.

These crises must, I believe, provoke the anxieties of loss, generating ideological bewilderment and conflicts which project the confusion of meaning. Yet because they grow gradually out of latent contradictions, they may be unrelated to any particular or obviously critical situation. Hence we cannot easily grasp the nature of the crisis, or even its inevitability, though the evidence of disintegration is all around us: and until we do, even the best intentions of reform will be shadowed by an overbearing sense of meaningless irrelevance.

VIII
THE MANAGEMENT OF CHANGE

The first two chapters of this essay set out its central theme: how loss disrupts our ability to find meaning in experience, and how grief represents the struggle to retrieve this sense of meaning when circumstances have bewildered or betrayed it. In the rest of the book, I have tried to explore and elaborate this theme. Though the examples are drawn mostly from my own research, they cover a wide range of situations where—in both willed and unwilling change—the analogy with bereavement seems to clarify the nature of the stresses and the reactions they evoke. Each example is intended only to illustrate how, if we look at situations in this light, a fundamentally similar crisis of reintegration seems to be working itself out in them all. I hope that anyone whose imagination has been caught, as mine has been, by the recurrence of this underlying pattern can apply it to their own experience: and that may be more useful than any practical conclusion I can draw from the argument.

But since it is not immediately obvious that understanding the nature of bereavement can lessen the pain of grief, nor that we would manage change differently if we were more sensitive to the element of loss, I want to suggest how this way of looking at change might influence what we do. I think there would still be a virtue in understanding, even if it changed nothing in our behaviour, just because we would then be better prepared to withstand the strain of change. But in practice, in all the examples I have discussed, the process of change could have been articulated less destructively. The difficulty is to generalise from these cases. Each is part of a history—a unique set of economic, social and political circumstances— through which the universal impulses of human behaviour work themselves out. Any implication I might draw from them —about the recognition of tribalism, the value of mourning rituals, the tolerance of ambiguity, the rejection of slum clearance as an instrument of social change, or the tendency of innovators towards self-defeating isolation—could be misleading in some other time and place. So rather than make any specific recommendations, let me try to describe where I think an understanding of loss could inform the choice of action.

In the first place, we need to discriminate those changes where a sense of bereavement is likely to be provoked. Some changes are merely equivalents or extensions of something already familiar: even radical technological innovations may be readily assimilable, so long as they are perceived only as better instruments of an established purpose. Some changes restore familiarity, like recovery from an illness. Some add skills and experiences, without sacrifice. Even changes which require a radical reorientation of life need not be disruptive, if they fulfil a purpose already pressing for expression. These changes are represented in the normal process of growing up. They are characteristically preceded by boredom and restlessness, as new concerns, not yet articulated or focused, begin to divest the present of importance. At any stage of life, a long suppressed ideal, a fundamental need of attachment may break through, exposing the triviality of habitual expectations and setting people on a new adventure, with an indifference to their past which seems almost reckless. These changes may generate great anxiety, because they make the future suddenly much less secure. But they are experienced as an overwhelming revitalisation of the meaning of life, not as bereavement. They evoke latent impulses of attachment, whose suppression has constricted the feelings we can learn to express. In this, I think, lies the extraordinary commitment of a revivalist movement or a serious love affair. Even if the hope is an illusion and the adventure ends in disappointment, a habit of self-limitation has been outgrown.

The analogy with bereavement does not fit these changes, because none involves the loss of important attachments. Nor does it fit disruptive changes, however severe, if the loss is obviously retrievable. The analogy applies rather to those situations where crucial purposes have been disorientated—either because an attachment has been broken, or because circumstances are too baffling to attach any purpose to them, or because purposes are brought into contradiction by the convergence of different aspects of life. Then arises the crisis whose forms I have tried to describe. Such crises can develop from voluntary as much as involuntary changes, as their unforeseen or discounted consequences and latent contradictions begin to work themselves out. The changes are not necessarily therefore less desirable or inevitable: but their outcome will depend on the sensitivity with which the crisis is managed.

Any serious bereavement impairs the ability to attach meaning to events, and hence to learn from them how to survive. At the same time, loss is usually threatening: the victims recognise that unless they learn to understand the situation and cope with it, they will be helpless to secure a tolerable future. The disorientation of purpose is therefore a source of profound anxiety, as well as desolation. It undermines the structure of meaning on which learning depends. In atomistic terms, learning can be described as consolidating sequences of behaviour which are rewarding. So long as there is a possibility of reward, behaviour will seek to find it. A starving man is not bereaved while he still clings, however faintly, to the hope of relief, and uses the last of his energy to reach it. The peculiarity of grief is the loss of faith in any possible reward. This sense of desolation arises from the frustration of attachments to particular relationships, or relationships of a particular kind, for which there seems to be no acceptable substitute. Whenever human purposes depend on relationships to other people —whether of love or friendship, power or status, security of belonging—the satisfaction of these purposes seems to fasten on a specific person, class or group of people, with whom they become identified. Hence the loss of these relationships seems irredeemable, because no substitute attachment would be equivalent.

Recovery from grief depends on restoring a sense that the lost attachment can still give meaning to the present, not on finding a substitute. The purpose and feeling it expressed has somehow to be abstracted from its past setting and reformulated so as to make present and future behaviour interpretable as rewarding. I have tried to illustrate how the bereaved seem to make this transition by incorporating the relationship and continuing its ideals. It cannot be treated simply as a rational process of learning to make the best of things, where grief is merely to be endured. The working out of grief is itself the central, most urgent task, because the bereaved cannot repair the ability to learn any meaningful ways of coping, until they have undertaken it. Once they have worked this out, they will find vitality and confidence for other purposes. In time, the old attachment may be edged further and further from the centre of life, as all purposes may change. But at the moment of loss, this seems scarcely conceivable, except as self-destructive betrayal of the meaning of past experience. In any severe bereavement, the restoration of the lost attachment absorbs most of the victim's energy. Even when the loss is peripheral, the sense of disorientation, of experience being drained of some part of its meaning, sets up a nagging anxiety. If this minor grief is ignored, I think it may be more upsetting, in unrecognised ways, than it need have been. Moving house, for instance, or taking a new job may involve the sacrifice of familiar relationships with neighbours, colleagues, a community whose interest one shared, and though the new house or job may be better, that does not overcome the need to mourn, at least a little, for the loss.

So whenever we impose disruptive changes on ourselves or others, we need to allow some kind of moratorium on other business, so that people can give their minds to repairing the thread of continuity in their attachments; and we should not burden ourselves with so many simultaneous changes that our emotional resilience becomes exhausted. There is some evidence that an accumulation of personal changes, even if they are all desired, can provoke a breakdown in health. For the same reason, familiar features of the social environment may be worth preserving, even if they have no other value. Conservationists are often ridiculed for wanting to keep old buildings or familiar landmarks which are neither beautiful nor historically important. But the townscape ought to reflect our need for continuity, and the more rapidly society changes, the less readily should we abandon anything familiar which can still be made to serve a purpose. Even if a sweeping redesign would be more efficient, more practical, more beautiful, even if those who used it would come to prefer it, I think we should still consider whether such abrupt discontinuities are worth the stresses they set up. There is a virtue in rehabilitating familiar forms which neither economic logic nor conventional criteria of taste can fully take into account, and we should at least recognise this, before we decide what to destroy.

Yet I do not think the argument of this book implies a conventionally conservative attitude towards change. It is concerned rather with the stresses which change can generate, and how the management of these changes may affect the outcome. But it does imply that the need to sustain the familiar attachments and understanding, which make life meaningful, is as profound as other basic human needs. Hence injustice, inequality, exploitation do not necessarily impel their victims to seek radical changes, even when they are clearly perceived and widespread. The revolutionary analysis has first to be incorporated in everyday life, as the most meaningful framework of expectation by which to interpret events and direct behaviour. Such a transformation of familiar assumptions about the world and one's place in it is profoundly disturbing. It is less threatening to believe that one's hardships can be relieved within the framework of the present structure. Hence the conservative assumption that society can assimilate demands, and need only make incremental accommodations without changing its basic principles, has a much wider appeal than the class interests its principles best further. So revolutionary changes are unlikely until the ideological paradigm has degenerated to the point where it can no longer provide a coherent set of assumptions by which to live, much as a scientific paradigm decays. And since the more privileged classes of society have a disproportionate influence over the maintenance and inculcation of ideological structures, I think they too must sense their ideological decay. So, as I discuss in the final section of this chapter, revolutionary change—at least when it is internally generated—is a response to loss of meaning as much as a struggle for power. I am concerned here, not with the circumstances which demand change, or the ideals change should realise, but with the processes by which we come to terms with it. And once we turn our attention to this process, the articulation of its transitional stages appears crucial. The more radical the changes which evolve, the more important this is: we need to recognise the element of bereavement, above all, in the process of a major reconstruction. For then the whole purpose of change may be aborted by the mishandling of loss.

Whether the crisis of disorientation affects only an individual, or a group, or society as a whole, it has a fundamentally similar dynamic. It provokes a conflict between contradictory impulses—to return to the past, and to forget it altogether. Each, in itself, would be ultimately self-destructive, either by denying the reality of present circumstances, or by denying the experience on which the sense of self rests. But their interaction forces the bereaved to search to and fro, until they are reconciled by reformulating and reintegrating past attachments. If this process fails, life becomes mummified in a phantasy of the past; or empty and meaningless behind a façade of purposive activity; or obsessed by the unresolved conflict in a permanent crisis. The length and intensity of the crisis, the risk that its resolution will be abortive, can be reduced by the way the conflict is articulated and contained within a supportive structure. But though the underlying analysis applies, I believe, to any experience of loss, the implications are different when the experience is shared. Then the internal personal conflict can be projected into collective behaviour, and may be institutionalised. In what follows, I will chiefly discuss such situations as these. But first it may be helpful to say a little more about the management of solitary bereavement.

HELPING THE BEREAVED

In an earlier chapter, following Geoffrey Gorer's argument, I suggested how mourning customs can help to articulate grief—expressing its impulses in symbolic acts, containing them within a recognised period of social withdrawal and setting a term for their resolution. These rites and gestures of remembrance continue a relationship with the dead into a world he no longer inhabits. They attenuate the loss and help to incorporate the meaning of the relationship in the continuing stream of life. I do not think that we can artificially revive rituals whose symbols represent a discarded conception of death and the after-life. But we can seek for secular equivalents of their supportive functions—as, for instance, memorials can express through some continuing activity or object the interests and ideals of the dead. Especially, the friends and family of the severely bereaved can help to sustain them through the working out of grief, by the continuity of their own relationship. The bereaved often seem to become isolated, because their former companions are embarrassed by grief and do not know how to respond. Some friends are over-assertive, assuming the task of managing the weak; some stay away, unwilling to face the awkward encounter when condolences must first be expressed, or fearful of demands; others become over-deferential and respectful of the status of bereavement. The bereaved themselves, struggling with ambivalent feelings, acutely aware of their vulnerable and unsettled social position, become more sensitive to tactless words and clumsy gestures which seem insincere, officious or slighting. At the same time, they understand much better than any of their comforters the nature of the crisis they have to work through. The most supportive friends, I think, are those who unobtrusively but persistently offer their companionship, responding to the needs of grief.

These needs include the celebration of the dead person—a recognition of what she or he meant, and still means, to their friends: to ignore them, as a subject too painful to be broached, can only make the working out of grief lonelier and more frightening. Yet the bereaved also need everyday companionship, when they can forget their loss—see a film, talk of their friends' affairs, feel that they are still part of an uninterrupted social world: they do not want to be continually reminded how wretched they must be, how unhappy their friends are on their behalf, or listen to expressions of grief that can only be less than their own. They need, rather, a sense of practical and unassuming support—that their friends understand the nature of the crisis, are ready to offer companionship and useful help whenever they can, and respect the ultimate privacy of grief, without obtruding into a struggle of conflicting emotions which their advice can do little to resolve. I think a stranger, who understands grief in general, and stands in an acknowledged therapeutic role, can probably give more support to the working out of grief itself. Because this support is, in a sense, impersonal, it does not threaten to pre-empt the personal resolution of the crisis: for the most part, it simply offers reassurance that the crisis is natural, that it will find a resolution in time.

This advice reflects the ambivalence of grief: to acknowledge loss, yet to continue habits of companionship which loss need not disrupt; to be supportive, and recognise the nature of the crisis, yet not to obtrude sympathetic advice and expressions of distress. At different times, at different moments within the same evening's conversation, the bereaved may look for one response more than another. But I think most people are tactful and sensitive enough to provide the bereaved with the companionship they need, if only they will try. Often, it seems from my own experience, they do not try, but remain paralysed before the task of writing a letter of condolence, drop the grief-stricken from their social engagements, and ignore their part in repairing the loss until the work has been done for them.

I have been writing of death. But these suggestions can, I think, be adapted to any severe personal loss—eviction from a home, dismissal from a job, rejection from a relationship whose meaning was important. If, as in divorce, the rupture may have been sought, it is not so much the lost relationship itself whose meaning needs to be retrieved, as the hopes and purposes it betrayed. The working out of grief is then a restoration of faith that such hopes are not futile; that one is not, after all, incapable of giving or receiving love. In all these crises, essentially the same needs of support arise, with the same sensitivity to the conflicting impulses which must gradually be reconciled.

COLLECTIVE LOSSES

Once we turn from involuntary traumatic losses to situations where loss is an aspect of other kinds of changes, and from the isolation of private grief to the shared experience of disruptive change, the working out of the crisis takes on another aspect.[1]

[1] Sometimes, of course, traumatic personal loss may also be experienced at once by many people. In 1973, for instance, a plane crash killed a party of holiday-makers from the same English vil-

For the ambivalence can now be projected in a social conflict, and though the situation may seem remote from any sense of personal tragedy, it still reflects in transmuted form the dynamics of grieving. Hence the conflict cannot be treated simply as a clash of interests: it expresses also a search for identity, whose demands are more ambiguous, evolving with the conflict itself. I have tried to show how the ambivalence of loss may be embodied in institutions, and how important it becomes then to protect these institutions from a premature resolution of the issues. The Ibo village associations were both a reassertion of parochial traditions, and the roots of a political party whose slogan was 'One Nigeria'. The movement for the Third World College at the University of California in Berkeley expressed both loyalty to a long history of discrimination, to a sense of separate identity born of suffering and exclusion, and a demand for the incorporation of that history in the established institutions of a prestigious university. Such movements are superficially inconsistent. How can one demand recognition for the intellectual status of a subject, while denying the university any right to interfere in the recruitment of staff and students, insisting on open enrolment from the ghetto? Or proclaim national unity while reinforcing local patriotic attachments? But just these are the crucial questions. They represent the conflicting impulses which must ultimately be reconciled, and the virtue of tribalism is to articulate them. Hence these tribal movements are at once a challenge to society at large, and a search for the meaning of one's own identity in the bewilderment of changing life-chances. If we interpret them crudely as an assertion of political interests, we mistake their ambiguity, assuming that people have already found what they are seeking.

The articulation of this conflict is therefore as crucial to assimilating social changes as mourning is to bereavement. Even if it were possible to foresee how interests might be balanced with the utmost fairness, everyone has still to work out in his or her own terms what it means to their particular attachments,

---

lage. Such a disaster bereaves a community, and the sharing of grief does, I think, affect its expression. But these are fortunately rare events, and I have not considered them here.

gradually reorienting their essential purposes. No one can resolve the crisis of reintegration on behalf of another, any more than friends can tell the bereaved how to make the best of it. Every attempt to pre-empt conflict, argument, protest by rational planning can only be abortive: however reasonable the proposed changes, the process of implementing them must still allow the impulse of rejection to play itself out. When those who have power to manipulate changes act as if they have only to explain, and, when their explanations are not at once accepted, shrug off opposition as ignorance or prejudice, they express a profound contempt for the meaning of lives other than their own. For the reformers have already assimilated these changes to their purposes, and worked out a reformulation which makes sense to them, perhaps through months or years of analysis and debate. If they deny others the chance to do the same, they treat them as puppets dangling by the threads of their own conceptions. When liberal white people propose reforms on behalf of black, men on behalf of women, rich for poor, even the most honourable intentions can be profoundly alienating, if they assume the identity of those they seek to help and tell them what their lives should mean. The presumption is, I think, more intimately threatening than indifference or hostility, and is bitterly resented. To be told the meaning of your life by others, in terms which are not yours, implies that your existence does not matter to them, except as it is reflected in their own.

All this suggests three principles for the management of change. First, the process of reform must always expect and even encourage conflict. Whenever people are confronted with change, they need the opportunity to react, to articulate their ambivalent feelings and work out their own sense of it. Second, the process must respect the autonomy of different kinds of experience, so that groups of people can organise without the intrusion of alien conceptions. Third, there must be time and patience, because the conflicts involve not only the accommodation of diverse interests, but the realisation of an essential continuity in the structure of meaning. Each of these principles corresponds with an aspect of grief, as a crisis of reintegration which can neither be escaped, nor resolved by anyone on behalf of another, nor hurried.

These principles are seldom recognised in practice. The agents of change are preoccupied with the powers they must respect, and once they have negotiated a politically viable proposal, become impatient to implement it. They will, I think, most often try to save themselves the time and energy of further conflict—co-opting agreeable representatives of public opinion, outmanoeuvring attempts at organised opposition, fragmenting criticism and overwhelming it with expert knowledge. Legitimate discussion is to be contained within a co-operative framework, defined by their own conception of the common interest—costs, benefits, priorities of need, profitability, expansion. Not that their proposal need be unintelligent or unfair, nor their evasion of confrontation partisan. But people cannot reconcile themselves to the loss of familiar attachments in terms of some impersonal utilitarian calculation of the common good. They have to find their own meaning in these changes before they can live with them. Hence the reformers must listen as well as explain, continually accommodating their design to other purposes, other kinds of experience, modifying and renegotiating, long after they would like to believe that their conception was finished. If they impatiently cut this process short, their reforms are likely to be abortive.

Suppose, for instance, that the changes involve the reorganisation of a firm, or the teaching in a school system. Everyone in the organisation has come to understand his or her job —the purposes it satisfied, its give and take, the loyalties and rivalries it implies—as a familiar pattern of relationships, on which they rely to interpret the events of the working day. This definition of their occupational identity represents the accumulated wisdom of how to handle the job, derived from their own experience and the experience of all who have had the job before or share it with them. Change threatens to invalidate this experience, robbing them of the skills they have learned and confusing their purposes, upsetting the subtle rationalisations and compensations by which they reconciled the different aspects of their situation. Most of these people have little part in the decisions which determine the policy of the organisation; but collectively, they have great power to subvert, constrain or ignore changes they do not accept, because, after all, they do the work. If innovation is imposed upon them, without the chance to assimilate it to their experience, to argue it out, adapt it to their own interpretation of their working lives, they will do their best to fend it off. The changes may be tamed into conformity with familiar routines, or segregated as an extraneous adjunct to the organisation. The reforms in the American school system, pioneered by community action agencies under the anti-poverty programme, were repeatedly emasculated by these tactics. Projects ramified around the system, in pre-school, after school, summer school programmes, without touching the heart of the reformer's intention—to draw teachers, pupils and parents together in mutual understanding and collaboration. Yet with rare exceptions, the teachers and those they taught were never involved in the preparation of these changes, or invited to argue out their merits (see Marris and Rein, 1967, pp. 58–70). Similarly, Tom Burns and G. M. Stalker here described how the attempt to convert small Scottish manufacturing firms to electronics foundered on the unwillingness to incorporate research and development laboratories within their structure. Like a thorn in the flesh, surrounded by inflamed antagonisms and a swollen tissue of mediators, the laboratories remained productively and often physically isolated (Burns and Stalker, 1961).

Reforms within organisations are vulnerable to these stultifying tactics, since the changes can only be carried out by those who resist them. People cannot so readily defend themselves against social changes which they are not required to promote. But if such changes, too, are imposed upon them without the opportunity to assimilate their meaning, the outcome may be even more damaging in the long run. People not only become alienated from the purposes of government, but from themselves. If the changes are disruptive and frequent, they must, I think, lose confidence that their own lives have a meaningful continuity of purpose. And this aimlessness or cynicism will still be provoked even if the changes are intelligent and necessary, so long as people cannot make sense of them in terms of their own experience.

The analogy between change and bereavement implies, then, a need to articulate conflict in subtler and more personal ways than the arbitration of interests can itself express. The process of change has to accommodate a politics of identity, which brings to that arbitration all the unresolved ambivalence of loss. If the evolution of the conflict is to help people work out some meaningful resolution, it must first make clearer to them and to others what crucial purposes and attachments seem threatened by change, and then explore how these purposes can be retrieved and reformulated in the particular context of individual experience. The conflict must therefore recognise the autonomy of experience, respecting the need of every group to find its own sense of continuity. There is, I think, in any important confrontation with disruptive changes, a hierarchy of conflicts, for each major division—between national and local, management and labour, organisation and client, black and white—contains within it sub-divisions, differences of experience and purpose which must also be argued out or segregated. If this hierarchy is not clearly articulated, conflicts at different levels confuse and weaken each other. So, for instance, a mayor may offer to negotiate with a community in his city, without allowing time for the community to resolve its internal differences apart from him, and then exploit this disarray to excuse the imposition of his own policy. I doubt if these tactics ever successfully forestall conflict, but they can stultify and demoralise it.

These inferences for the management of change are not at all specific—even conflict itself should be understood loosely, to mean any confrontation from outright opposition to argument or the assertion of a group identity. The forms in which internal tensions can be relieved and worked out through collective action will vary too much with circumstances for me to elaborate them here. But these kinds of conflict are, I believe, distinctively different from more obvious conflicts of interest, and fulfil a partly different need. They are concerned with the search for meaning; and meaning may be found in a fair settlement, in institutions which sustain conflicts of interest which have now become clear, in the definition of ideological opposition, or simply in understanding that what must be given up is not, after all, vital. They merge into political action, but are also expressions of mourning, in the sense that they give meaningful structure to a process of transition whose outcome is still clouded by ambivalence.

Imagine, as an analogy, a homogeneous society where mourning is highly ritualised—a traditional African tribe, for instance. The rituals dramatise a sequence of acts, which separate the dead person from the rights and duties attributed to him or her, so that these attributes may be reinstated and continued, in their name or the name of their kinsmen. So the meaning of lineage, as the framework of purpose—the thread of continuity which unites the living, the dead and the still unborn—is reaffirmed. Relationships and statuses are redefined in this affirmation, but not all at once. Grieving itself becomes a meaningful part to play, whose purpose is to work out, step by step, this delicate abstraction of the continuity of life from the particular attachments in which it must always somehow be embodied. Hence, I think, the bereaved are less bewildered and disoriented, their recovery from grief more secure: and this does not depend upon their knowing—or upon anyone else necessarily knowing—exactly how their fate will finally be settled.

It seems to me that the conflicts I have tried to describe have comparable qualities. They, too, provide a gradual transition, in which the victims of loss can find a meaningful role, without needing to know how the conflict will come out. Conflict is a powerful organising principle of behaviour, defining friends and enemies, good and bad, in terms of immediate, transitory purposes. At the same time, it relieves the internal tensions of loss by displacing ambivalence onto an opponent, whose resistance restrains impulses which could not otherwise be so single-mindedly expressed without being self-destructive. The opposition, that is, represents aspects of the need to conserve the past, or realise a different future, which the other side can then afford not to acknowledge, though it shares them, since each constrains the other's recklessness. So, like mourning, the conflict dramatises a transition, and makes the transition itself a meaningful sequence of actions, without needing to prescribe the forms of accommodation to which it leads. Thus the working out of grief is projected as negotiation, through which everyone will come to reformulate their own sense of the meaning of their situation—whether in agreement or division. But just as mourning rituals presuppose a shared understanding of life and death, so in more complex heterogeneous societies, the conflicts must be expressed in terms of the shared experience of each distinct group.

I do not mean to suggest that conflicts which represent a struggle for power and those which represent a struggle for meaning are separate events. They merge into each other. The process of coming to terms with loss may well begin by testing whether loss has to be accepted, and the power to defend the meaning of one's life against the disruptions of change is itself a reflection of the distribution of resources. In tracing the analogies between bereavement and change, I have looked only at one aspect of events. But I believe that unless we understand how one conflict may underlie the other, how the arbitration of interests may only be possible once grief has been worked out, we will not know how to articulate humane processes of change.

Complex industrial societies have, I think, an especial need to find forms in which such conflicts can be expressed. Their economic organisation is at once so highly differentiated, so tightly integrated over so wide a range of places and functions, and so dependent on competitive innovation that the repercussions of frequent changes hammer insistently at the familiar structure of people's lives. As Donald Schon writes (1971, pp. 27–8):

> Individuals must somehow confront and negotiate, in their own persons, the transformations which used to be handled by generational change . . . while technological change has been continuing exponentially for the last two hundred years, it has now reached a level of pervasiveness and frequency uniquely threatening to the stable state.

And these technological changes cannot be isolated from the social relationships in which they are embedded. An apparently discreet innovation, such as the introduction of hybrid maize, may undermine a whole tradition of peasant life, as it did in France.

Businesses can adapt to this instability by abstracting their organisation from commitment to any particular product or technology. The most successful evolve sophisticated structures able to assimilate a wide variety of demands and tech-

niques. But they can only do so because they set themselves an
equally abstract purpose, the maximising of their profit over
time. Their human counterpart is the rational man of economic theory, who seeks the same end. But in reality, our attachments are specific: we love particular people, places, kinds
of work, and cannot readily substitute for them by any abstract calculus of generalised well-being. If we try to adapt by
inhibiting our need for these enduring attachments we fail to
realise a satisfying meaning to our lives, dogged by an uneasy
sense of loneliness, and nagging doubt of who we really are.
Hence we have continually to defend our personal lives
against a style of organisation which is adaptive only for the
large-scale corporations which dominate the economy and
have learned to flourish on its changeability. Unless people
can react articulately to this continual threat of disintegration,
their sense of loss will turn inward in apathy, depression,
cynicism, guilt and violence.

Thus institutions, both public and private, try to assimilate
the consequences of large-scale, highly differentiated and
densely integrated systems by evolving management structures
of comparable breadth. To do so, they must reformulate their
purposes at a level of abstraction which increases the range of
meaningful purposes open to them. As corporations divorce
their strategy from commitment to a product, so government
seeks to divorce its management from traditional, narrowly
defined departmental functions. But this response has to contend with the fundamental need to protect, in our personal
lives, the possibility of specific lasting attachments. Hence we
are driven to defend, more and more anxiously, the stability of
our immediate social environment against collective decisions
over which we have scarcely any control. In reaction against
the scale and abstraction of government, we set up tribal and
territorial boundaries to withstand the threat to the meaning of
our lives. This conflict cannot be reconciled by the rules of rep-
resentative democracy, which at best only articulates a highly
aggregated opposition of interests. It represents a more fundamental conflict between contradictory adaptive responses,
which can only be worked out through a pervasive and insistent process of confrontation and negotiation. This, I believe,
is the crucial problem of modern government. We cannot solve

it merely by more sensitive and responsive planning procedures. We have to take the conflict as the central issue, and evolve from it a new conception of democracy.

This would be the subject for another book. Here I have only tried to show how the analysis of loss leads towards a radical revision of government.

REVOLUTIONARY CHANGE

Several people who read this essay in draft asked how I would relate the argument to revolutionary change. I have no experience of such changes from my own research, through which to apply the argument in any detail. But I should explain, firstly, why the idea of revolution does not contradict the basic assumptions of my argument; and this leads to some general conclusions about the characteristic dilemma of revolutionary reconstructions. The discussion treats revolutions as generated within society, neither externally imposed, nor replacing an external authority; and though this is a simplification, I think much of it would still apply, with qualification, to colonial situations.

The idea of revolution may seem, at first sight, to deny the need for continuity. It suggests a new beginning, where the meaning of all relationships derives from an ideology independent of the preceding society. In this sense, it resembles a religious conversion, where the convert is symbolically reborn, and has revealed to him a wholly new meaning to experience. Is it possible, then, to undergo radical, disruptive changes, yet without grief, to put on a ready-made identity like a new suit of clothes? If so, all that I have written about the conservative impulse, and the dependence of learning on continuity of purpose and predictable relationships would have to be much qualified. But I think the analysis of revolutions would show instead that they are continually and urgently preoccupied with questions of identity, with the search for continuity and the reformulation of purpose, in a manner as far-reaching and troubled as the changes they represent.

It seems misleading, in the first place, to regard revolutions as themselves the primary disruptive events. They happen when the meaning of life has already disintegrated, and succeed when such disintegration has confused and demoralised so many classes of society that no coherent collective will to defend the past survives. Thus they represent a response to that sense of bereavement which follows when latent contradictions in the understanding of relationships become manifest and inseparable. Such loss can occur at any level of social organisation. A woman learns that her husband has been having an affair: nothing has overtly changed in their relationship, but his adultery may seem to her irreconcilable with the meaning she has given to her marriage, and the anomaly bereaves her. Friend and enemy may merge in the same person, undermining the meaning of war. Or, as I discussed earlier, incompatible principles of education may evolve side by side, until their contradictions can no longer be ignored. Revolutions arise, I suppose, above all from contradictions and anomalies in economic and political relationships, and in societies where the will to master those contradictions has been weakened by military or economic invasion. But it seems likely that confusions at this level would provoke and aggravate anomalous situations at every level, pervading society with a troubled, inexplicit sense of loss. So, for instance, the characters in a Chekhov play seem to prefigure the Russian Revolution in the whole texture of their lives.

Thomas Kuhn's analysis of scientific revolutions as the attrition and usurpation of paradigms seems to me closely analogous to the process of political revolution. Both kinds of revolution arise from the internal decay of the preceding construction of reality; both are characteristically, if not necessarily, first formulated long before the established order has exhausted its attempts to rationalise the anomalies and contradictions within its own framework; and both are ultimately accepted when these rationalisations seem to lead to a dead end. I have tried to show earlier how, in Kenya, both repression and liberalisation weakened the colonial structure, because they alike heightened the inherent contradictions of colonial ideology. Repression became morally repugnant to British opinion as its brutalities were exposed, undermining conviction in the legitimacy of the colonial mission. Liberal constitutions conceded the principle of democracy without the fact, raising expectations which they did not satisfy, but could not convincingly deny. Hence independence—which ten years before had seemed to nearly all colonial officials a remote outcome inconceivable for another generation—became the only meaningful way of reconstructing society. And this came about despite the successful military suppression of revolt.

De Tocqueville shows how the French Revolution arose from the disintegration of feudal institutions—not in the nations where these institutions were most oppressive, but in the nation which had already, in practice, largely abandoned them. Many of the most important achievements ascribed to the Revolution—the break-up of the landed estates, the centralisation of an administration staffed by career civil servants, the growth of independent peasant landowners—had already come about: it was the inability of the old regime to incorporate such changes coherently that made revolution inevitable. As de Tocqueville says (1966 edn, p. 51):

> Chance played no part whatever in the outbreak of the Revolution; though it took the world by surprise, it was the inevitable outcome of a long period of gestation, the abrupt and violent conclusion of a process in which six generations had played an intermittent part. Even if it had not taken place, the old social structure would nonetheless have been shattered everywhere sooner or later. The only difference would have been that instead of collapsing with such brutal suddenness it would have crumbled bit by bit. At one fell swoop, without warning, without transition, and without compunction, the Revolution effected what in any case was bound to happen, if by slow degrees.

The endeavours of the old regime to reorganise the social structure themselves created the pervasive disorientation against which revolution reacted (ibid., p. 220):

> When the Revolution broke out, that part of the government which, though subordinate, keeps every citizen aware of its existence and affects his daily life at every turn, had just been thrown into confusion; the public administration had made a clean sweep of all its former representatives and embarked on a quite new programme. Radical as they were, these reforms did not seem to have jeopardised the State itself, but every Frenchman was affected by them, if only in a

minor way. He felt that his life had somehow been disor-
ganised, that he must cultivate new habits, and if a businessman, that his activities would now be handicapped.
True, routine of a kind still prevailed in the conduct of
affairs of vital importance to the nation, but already no one
knew from whom he should take orders, to whom he should
apply, or how to solve those small private problems which
crop up almost daily in the life of every member of a social
group.

While the old regime was struggling ineffectually to reconcile reform with tradition, men of letters, in isolation from government, were elaborating a fundamentally different theory of
society (ibid., p. 167):

> Thus alongside the traditional and confused, not to say
> chaotic, social system of the day there was gradually built
> up in men's minds an imaginary ideal society in which all
> was simple, uniform, coherent, equitable, and rational in the
> full sense of the term. It was this vision of the perfect State
> that fired the imagination of the masses and little-by-little es-
> tranged them from the here-and-now.

The French Revolution, in its conception, was a metaphor of
great power, whose influence on our perception of society
remains to this day.

Yet at the same time, it incorporated many of the institutions already created, discarding essentially those feudal and
aristocratic remnants most obviously incongruous with the
realities of contemporary society. And as the Revolution
evolved into the Napoleonic regime, it even restored the continuity of aristocratic symbols. Hence its importance lies not in
the inevitable changes of which it was the historical instrument, but the sense it made of them. Like a new scientific
theory, it reformulated meaning, and set the direction of purposeful experiment for the future: and, indeed, the great revolutionary theories present themselves as science—a supremely
rational interpretation of the relationship between a fundamental ethic and its social realisation.

An analysis very similar to de Tocqueville's would surely
apply to the Russian Revolution—the progressive disintegra-

tion of the old regime, its inability to incorporate liberal reforms and economic changes coherently within its structure, the pervasive disorientation provoked by military defeat, and the eventual reconstruction of many Tsarist institutions within the Soviet state. Lenin at the Finland Station did not hold the forces to dominate the Revolution, but he held it in his intellectual grasp, unrivalled in his skill to reconcile every pragmatic adjustment with a coherent, indomitable theory of revolutionary purpose.

The Chinese and Cuban Revolutions of our time also came at the end of a century of confusion and disintegration. Both appear as the culmination of a succession of abortive revolutionary endeavours which failed to establish a meaningful social reconstruction. This ineffectuality of meaning, rather than repression or inequality itself, seems to provoke further revolution: for repressive and unjust regimes, like the South African, seem all too secure while their ruling classes remain convinced of their ideological justification. The triumph of the Chinese and Cuban Revolutions could not have been predicted from the balance of force. In Cuba, especially, Castro's strength grew from the defection of the middle class, as Batista frustrated every attempt at liberal reform, his government degenerating into a style with which fewer and fewer could identify. Batista was still in the militarily stronger position when he fled.

I hope these brief references are enough to suggest how revolutionary changes might be brought within the framework of my argument. The coherence of a social structure begins to disintegrate under the pressure of anomalies and contradictions it cannot assimilate, and as it does so, more and more relationships become confused, irregular and difficult to identify. People experience a sense of loss, and try at once to reassert the past and escape into an idealised, detached vision of the future. Each is an impractical solution to their present distress: but the interaction of these contradictory impulses, like the working out of grief, gradually abstracts and reformulates from past experience a viable reconstruction of meaningful relationships. But where society is too fragmented, or its central authority too severely damaged—often by intrusion from abroad—tentative reconstructions only weaken still further the outworn shell of government which tries to incorporate them. Then only a political revolution can create the framework to contain them—the decisive step in a process of reintegration. It may still have to contend with reactionary movements, which seek to restore threatened privileges. But these movements no longer represent a meaningful conception of society. Unless they are powerfully supported from outside, they are, I think, bound to remain weak and unstable. Since they cannot secure consent, they exhaust their energies in ever-growing repression. This model of revolutionary change is only intended as a simplified outline, which in any historical situation would surely contain many political cross-currents. (Nor, of course, is any transfer of power necessarily revolutionary, in this sense. A military *coup d'état,* or independence from colonial rule, need not change the underlying structure of social relationships, nor the ideology which represents it, though the implications of the transfer may in time become impossible to assimilate.) The revolution succeeds because it promises absolute meaning, and that is the most urgent need. Hence the enthusiasm and revitalisation of purpose it generates at its outset, and the ruthlessness with which it sweeps aside everything that stands in its way.

Yet this must present the revolution with a daunting task. Since it imposes a new theory of society, every social relationship has to be reinterpreted in the light of it—between men and women, parents and children, workers and managers, artists and their public, as well as relationships of political control. These reinterpretations must be both experimental and convincing, for the revolution will be demoralised unless the predictability of relationships is quickly restored, while no one can foresee what will work in practice. Hence I do not mean to suggest that a revolution, in fact, satisfactorily resolves from its outset the problems of meaning: rather, like a new scientific theory, it asserts confidently that they can be solved, that the anomalies it presents are not intractable, as they were within the former structure of society. It has, therefore, to work out forms of government which at once defend the theory from any challenge, while it experiments pragmatically with coherent ways of implementing it in every aspect of life. The revolu tion becomes a great teacher, and every class of society with an acknowledged place in its future is absorbed in the process of learning its new identity. If the teaching is too clumsy and authoritarian, it will reactivate the sense of loss, plunging people again into helpless bewilderment. So every revolution must, I think, be beset by the risks of its dilemma: if it is too openly experimental, it may be overwhelmed by the chaos of different interpretations; if it is too dogmatic, it destroys once again the meaning which people have begun to work out—even the people themselves—in a brutal persecution of unorthodoxy. And in this dilemma, it may be tempted to revive more and more of the institutions and ideology of the old society, because these familiar habits of thought and relationship are readily intelligible, where they can be glossed over with a revolutionary justification.

In his account of the Revolution in a Chinese village in 1946–8 William Hinton (1966) describes these strains in moving details. Who, exactly, was a landlord, middle peasant, poor peasant? The meaning of the revolution had to be worked out in the sharing of a donkey, the division of a field, the reconstruction of village government, and despite weeks or months of debate, attempts at reformulation were repeatedly discredited. At first the poor peasants received too little, then too much. The Party agents were called to account for alienating the middle-class allies of the Revolution, and nearly demoralised by the painful duty to acknowledge their mistakes. New village leaders were required to confess abuses of power. But these re-examinations were conducted with extraordinary patience, rarely breaking down in bullying or violence. Everyone was to understand their position, to see for themselves where they had gone wrong. The revolutionary process was conceived as a heroic exercise in self-education—sustained by strong commitment, though sometimes deeply frustrating—through which its theory would become practice in the smallest detail of everyday life. Those who guided it seem to have understood that the most urgent and fundamental revolutionary task was to enable everyone to find this meaning and incorporate it into their sense of their own identity.

Not that the process is ever complete. As the Chinese Revolution was consolidated, it seems to have drifted back towards traditional patterns of bureaucratic and intellectual élitism. As Hinton says (1970, p. 217):

> The victory of 1949, it is now clear, had by no means ended the class struggle in China; it had only transformed it. Having resolved, at least internally, the great contradiction between the Chinese people—primarily the workers and peasants—on the one hand, and the feudal landlords, the bureaucratic-comprador capitalists of the Kuomintang, and the American imperialists on the other, victory shifted a previously subordinate contradiction to the centre of the stage. This was the contradiction between the working class and the bourgeoisie, including the national bourgeoisie which was still an important component of new democratic society. The red thread of this new conflict ran through every sphere of Chinese life and every aspect of China's reconstruction. It took the form of a contest between the 'capitalist road' and the 'socialist road', in farming, in industry, in trade, in education, in culture, in politics.

The Cultural Revolution was, perhaps, less a deliberate act of policy than the outcome of anomalies which threatened once again to undermine the structure of social meaning. So, at least, it appears from William Hinton's later account (1972) of the disintegration of Tsinghua, China's foremost technological university, in 1966–8. The professors had effectively controlled the university's policy. Their commitment to the Revolution was sincere enough, but they assumed that scientific knowledge was indifferent to ideology. They used the texts and methods of exposition they had acquired in Russian or American schools, adopted a similar conception of their professional status, and similar criteria of intellectual achievement. To their students, these practices seemed irrelevant, authoritarian, and alien to the revolutionary culture in which they had grown up. This inconsistency provoked them to challenge the university authorities. Characteristically, the first response attempted to defend authority while making a show of concessions, and only compounded the frustrations. The university then disintegrated: the professors retreated into hiding, the most militant students formed into two rival camps, barricaded in the buildings of the campus, while the rest scattered to their homes.

These remaining students were intensely concerned to restore the meaning of the Revolution. Both sides saw themselves in terms of its tradition: the threat of capitalism had revived, and it was up to them to beat it down as the loyal children of Mao Tse-tung. So, as I would expect in a period of acute disorientation, they projected the conflict. But partly because the professors had withdrawn and the students only confronted each other, partly because external political authority was distracted and divided by a general upheaval, the conflict was too isolated and introverted to articulate the real issue—how students were to reconcile their revolutionary and professional identities. Hence it degenerated into a fanatical and increasingly violent internal war, as poster campaigns and slander gave way to torture, shooting and arson. Each camp came to believe the other to be a reincarnation of the Kuomintang, though all that really divided them were personalities, the grievances of their mutual abuses, and the need to act out the tensions of their ambivalence. Hence they fell readily under the influence of the most intransigent and self-confident leaders.

At last, with great dignity, reasoning and restraint, despite savage provocations to violence, the workers of Pekin invaded the campus. They established the same patient process of re-education and reconstruction as Hinton had described in an obscure village twenty years before: only now the ordinary people were guiding the intellectuals. These events seem to represent the whole revolutionary sequence in microcosm—intolerable contradictions lead to ineffectual reforms which produce the final breakdown, and the revolutionary reconstruction comes only at the end, as the ambivalence of loss wears itself out.

Thus political and scientific revolutions alike seem to evolve from the internal decay of meaningful structures. But the disintegration of social meaning encounters more anxious resistance, evokes a deeper and more intimate sense of loss, since it involves the attachments of our everyday lives; and we confront it without the supporting logic of a scientific method.

A political revolution is reintegrative rather than disruptive, unless it is imposed by external force upon a society still confident of its meaning. It bereaves only those to whom it seems to offer no possible future identity. For most people, the revolution resolves the conflicts of loss, reinterpreting both past and future so as to restore a thread of continuity, a sense of abiding human purpose. Like a scientific theory, it incorporates past experience, but sets it in a radically different framework of explanation, which promises a better sense to the continuing experiment of living in society. Though it too will evolve, and uncover its own contradictions, it is a fundamental, irreversible restructuring of reality.

The analogy helps too, I think, to place revolutionary ideas within a comparatively stable society. Suppose that most people can make tolerable sense of their lives. They are more or less aware of all manner of injustice, stupidity, ugliness, contradiction—the anomalies which cannot be convincingly reconciled with the prevailing conception of society and how it works. But some they ignore as trivial, others they evade by segregating different aspects of life, applying to each incompatible structures of interpretation; others, again, they trust can be resolved in time, within the existing framework of thought. Society evolves like a scientific paradigm which has not yet exhausted the vitality of its metaphor—its power to generate meaningful experiments, to resolve puzzles and extend the scope of its principles. Yet within that society, there will be people for whom the paradigm has already broken down, who cannot see how the anomalies might ever be dealt with in its terms, nor evade the issue in their personal lives. For them, revolutionary ideas are the only framework capable of restoring a sense of meaning. And they may be right, in the sense that the prevailing theory of society may be ultimately untenable. But the practical question is not its truth, but whether it has yet outlived its potential as a direction of enquiry. Until then, the idea of revolution is the alternative hypothesis: and the acknowledgement that such an alternative has been put forward, that the majority for the time being reject its logic, itself becomes absorbed into the structure of meaning. Thus revolutionary ideas evolve their own tradition within the social structure which rejects them, as a counterpoint to its theory, and each defines itself in opposition to the other. I would guess that the better this interaction is articulated, the less abrupt and shattering will be the transition from one to the other.

REFERENCES

BETTELHEIM, BRUNO (1961) *The Informed Heart*, London, Thames & Hudson.

BOWLBY, JOHN (1961) 'Process of mourning', *International Journal of Psychoanalysis*, vol. XLII, Part 4/5, pp. 319–20.

— (1970) 'Self reliance and some conditions that promote it', paper read at a scientific meeting to mark the Tavistock Clinic Jubilee, September.

BURNS, TOM and STALKER, G. M. (1961) *The Management of Innovation*, London, Tavistock Publications.

CARMICHAEL, STOKELEY and HAMILTON, CHARLES V. (1969) *Black Power*, Harmondsworth, Penguin.

CAUTE, DAVID (1970) *Fanon*, London, Collins Fontana.

DICKENS, CHARLES (1970) *Dombey and Son*, ed. Peter Fairclough, Harmondsworth, Penguin.

DOUGLAS, MARY (1966) *Purity and Danger*, London, Routledge & Kegan Paul.

FANON, FRANZ (1968) *Les Damnés de la terre*, Paris, François Maspero.

FLAVELL, JOHN H. (1963) *The Developmental Psychology of Jean Piaget*, London, Van Nostrand Reinhold.

FREUD, SIGMUND (1925) 'Mourning and melancholia', in *Collected Papers*, vol. IV, London, Hogarth Press.

FRIED, MARC (1963) 'Grieving for a lost home', in *The Urban Condition*, ed. Leonard Duhl, New York, Basic Books.

GANS, HERBERT (1962) *The Urban Villagers*, New York, Free Press.

GARFINKEL, HAROLD (1967) *Studies in Ethnomethodology*, New York, Prentice Hall.

GEERTZ, CLIFFORD (1963) *Pedlars and Princes: Social Development and Economic Change in Two Indonesian Towns,* University of Chicago Press.

GOODY, JACK (1962) *Death, Property and the Ancestors,* London, Tavistock Publications.

GORER, GEOFFREY (1965) *Death, Grief and Mourning in Contemporary Britain,* London, Cresset Press.

GUGLER, JOSEF (1970) 'Life in a dual system: Eastern Nigerians in town 1961', in *Urban Growth in Subsaharan Africa,* ed. Josef Gugler, Nkanga Series No. 6, Makerere Institute of Social Research.

HAGEN, EVERETT (1964) *On the Theory of Social Change,* London, Tavistock Publications.

HEUSSLER, ROBERT (1963) *Yesterday's Rulers: the Making of the British Colonial Service,* Syracuse University Press.

HILL, CHRISTOPHER (1970) *God's Englishman,* Harmondsworth, Penguin.

HINTON, WILLIAM (1966) *Fanshen,* New York, Vintage Books.

— (1970) *Iron Oxen,* New York, Vintage Books.

— (1972) *Hundred Day War,* New York, Monthly Review Press.

HUDSON, LIAM (1970) 'Personality and scientific aptitude', in *The Ecology of Human Intelligence,* ed. Liam Hudson, Harmondsworth, Penguin Books.

KENYATTA, JOMO (1938) *Facing Mount Kenya,* London, Secker & Warburg.

KOESTLER, ARTHUR (1964) *The Act of Creation,* London, Hutchinson.

KUHN, THOMAS S. (1970) 'The essential tension: tradition and innovation in scientific research', in *The Ecology of Human Intelligence,* ed. Liam Hudson, Harmondsworth, Penguin.

LAKATOS, IMRE (1970) 'Methodology of scientific research programmes', in *Criticism and the Growth of Knowledge,* ed. I. Lakatos and A. Musgrave, Cambridge University Press.

LAKATOS, IMRE and MUSGRAVE, ALAN, eds (1970) *Criticism and the Growth of Knowledge,* Cambridge University Press.

LEARY, TIMOTHY (1968) *High Priest,* New York, New American Library.

LEGUM, COLIN (1966) 'The Massacre of the Proud Ibos', *Observer,* 16 October.

LEWIS, C. S. (1961) *A Grief Observed,* London, Faber & Faber.

LINDEMANN, ERICH (1944) 'Symptomatology and management of acute grief', *American Journal of Psychiatry,* vol. 101, September.

LLOYD, PETER (1955) 'The Yoruba lineage', *Africa.*

MC CLELLAND, DAVID (1961) *The Achieving Society*, New York, Van Nostrand.

MARRIS, PETER (1958) *Widows and their Families*, London, Routledge & Kegan Paul.

— (1961) *Family and Social Change in an African City*, London, Routledge & Kegan Paul.

— (1964) *The Experience of Higher Education*, London, Routledge & Kegan Paul.

MARRIS, PETER and REIN, MARTIN (1967) *Dilemmas of Social Reform*, London, Routledge & Kegan Paul.

MARRIS, PETER and SOMERSET, ANTHONY (1971) *African Businessmen*, London, Routledge & Kegan Paul.

MARSDEN, DENNIS (1969) *Mothers Alone*, London, Allen Lane.

MASLOW, ABRAHAM (1968) *Towards a Psychology of Being*, New York, Van Nostrand.

MERTON, ROBERT K. (1970) 'The role of genius in scientific advance', in *The Ecology of Human Intelligence*, ed. Liam Hudson, Harmondsworth, Penguin.

MORISON, ELTING (1964) *Men, Machines and Modern Times*, Cambridge, Mass., M.I.T. Press.

MURRAY PARKES, COLIN (1965) 'Bereavement and mental illness', *British Journal of Medical Psychology*, vol. 38, No. 1, p. 1.

— (1971) 'Psycho-social transitions: a field for study', *Social Science and Medicine*, vol. 5, p. 104.

OKAFOR-OMALI, DILIM (1965) *A Nigerian Villager in Two Worlds*, London, Faber & Faber.

OPIE, I. and P. (1959) *The Lore and Language of School Children*, Oxford, The Clarendon Press.

PARKES, JAMES (1955) 'The history of the Anglo-Jewish community', in *A Minority in Britain*, ed. Maurice Freedman, London, Vallentine, Mitchell.

PARLETT, M. R. (1970) 'The syllabus bound student', in *The Ecology of Human Intelligence*, ed. Liam Hudson, Harmondsworth, Penguin.

ROSBERG, CARL and NOTTINGHAM, JOHN (1966) *The Myth of Mau Mau: Nationalism in Kenya*, New York, Praeger.

SCHON, DONALD (1971) *Beyond the Stable State*, London, Temple Smith.

SCHWAB, WILLIAM B. (1958) 'The terminology of kinship and marriage amongst the Yoruba', *Africa*.

SMILES, SAMUEL (1862) *Lives of Engineers*, London, John Murray.

STERN, KARL; WILLIAMS, GWENDOLYN and PRADOS, MIGUEL (1965) 'Grief reactions in later life', in *Death and Identity*, ed. Robert Fulton, New York, John Wiley.

TOCQUEVILLE, ALEXIS DE (1850) *The Ancient Regime and the French Revolution,* trans. Stuart Gilbert, London, Collins Fontana, 1966.

WARREN, ROLAND C. (1971) *Truth, Love and Social Change,* New York, Rand, McNally.

WEAVER, ROBERT (1963) 'Major factors in urban planning', in *The Urban Condition,* ed. Leonard Duhl, New York, Basic Books.

WILLMOTT, PETER (1963) *Evolution of a Community,* London, Routledge & Kegan Paul.

YOUNG, MICHAEL and WILLMOTT, PETER (1957) *Family and Kinship in East London,* London, Routledge & Kegan Paul.

INDEX

Accents, as social barriers, 84–5

Adaptation, basic principles, 11, 141; and conflict, 164–73; and conservative impulse, 3, 7–22

African businessmen in Kenya: educational frustrations, 113–14, 150; motives, 112–17; organisational difficulties, 118–21

Ambivalence: of grief, 31–3, 35, 102, 162, 164; of tribal institutions, 77–81, 165

Amin, Idi, 81n

Army, regimental loyalties, 86n

Asian businessmen: African attitude towards, 118; attitude to Kenyan citizenship, 80

Asians: in Kenya, 79–81; political handicaps, 122; stereotypes of, 79; in Uganda, 81n

Azikiwe, Nnamdi, 69

Balinese aristocracy, 122

Batista, Fulgencio, 177

Bereavement: compared to divorce, 43–4; help in, 162–4; and loss of meaning, 25, 36–8; prospective, 115; situations of, 132–3, 158–60; *see also* Grieving, Mourning

Berkeley, University of California, 87–8, 165

Bettelheim, Bruno, 15, 17

Boston, 47, 60

Boston Redevelopment Authority, 47

Bowlby, John, 22, 32–3n

Brindley, James, 126

Burns, Tom, 168

Cambridge University, student stereotypes, 83–4, 85–6

Carmichael, Stokeley, 103

Castro, Fidel, 177

Caute, David, 101

Change: in complex industrial societies, 171–2; as loss and growth, 22–5

Chekhov, Anton, 174

Chick, Mrs, 16

Chinese Revolution, 177, 179–81

Citizenship of Kenya Asians, 80–1

Civil Service, and tribal balance, 76–7

Colonial policy: in Kenya, 145–51; towards recruitment, 15, 17

Commonwealth Immigration Act, 81

Communists, 15

Community action: and management of conflict, 105–7, 169; in schools, 168

Community groups, coalitions, 108

Concentration camps, Nazi, 15, 17

Conflict: and assimilation of change, 166; of grief reactions, 31–2; as mourning, 170; as rationalisation of grief, 102; as response to loss, 104–8, 165–73; of roles, 133, 155

Conservation, 160

Conservative impulse: adaptiveness of, 8–12, 14–21; defined, 4, 10–11; and frustra-